Complexi Financial Markets

EDGAR E. PETERS

John Wiley & Sons, Inc.

New York • Chichester • Weinheim • Brisbane • Singapore • Toronto

Copyright © 1999 by Edgar E. Peters. All rights reserved.

Published by John Wiley & Sons, Inc.

Published simultaneously in Canada.

This publication is designed to provide accurate and authoritative information in regard to the subject matter covered. It is sold with the understanding that the publisher is not engaged in rendering legal, accounting, or other professional services. If professional advice or other expert assistance is required, the services of a competent professional person should be sought.

Library of Congress Cataloging in Publication Data:
Peters, Edgar E., 1952–
    Patterns in the dark: understanding risk and financial crisis with complexity theory / Edgar E. Peters.
        p.   cm. — (Wiley investment series)
    Includes bibliographical references and index.
    ISBN 0-471-23947-X (cloth : alk. paper)
    ISBN 0-471-39981-7 (paper : alk. paper)
    1. Free enterprise.   2. Austrian school of economics.   I. Title.
II. Series
HB95.P42   1999
330.15'7—dc21   97-52583

Printed in the United States of America

10   9   8   7   6   5   4   3   2   1

*To my children Ian and Lucia, who taught me
more than they know, and*

*To the memory of Dr. Richard A. Crowell,
mentor, colleague, and friend.*

. . . they are looking in utter darkness for that which has no existence whatsoever.

—Desiderius Erasmus

Preface

WE know that things are uncertain at times of crisis. Uncertainty disrupts financial markets. It induces mob behavior. People hate uncertainty. Often, there is a feeling that a conspiracy must be behind it all, organizing and disseminating the problems. Someone must be punished. The witches must be burned. The communist spies must be revealed. People begin looking for signs of the conspiracy, particularly events which, when connected, will reveal a tapestry of deception—a pattern that will be there for all to see.

If we look hard enough, we can always find a pattern. Experts will say that the "probability" that a particular connection might happen by chance is very small. Most of their readers or listeners will take the qualified statement as a proclamation of truth, though it is never made clear how probabilities for such events can be calculated. In retrospect, the conspiracies usually turn out to be deadly flights of the imagination. There are no witches. There was no communist conspiracy. Yet the patterns were there. What was it that we were seeing?

In nature and in social systems, there are many processes that self-organize; that is, independent elements spontaneously begin cooperating and acting as one entity without an organizer. In the weather, we see these processes as hurricanes or tornadoes. In social systems, they have been variously described as bull markets, the "invisible hand" of the free markets, or the madness of mobs. In the sciences, the study of *complex systems* has identified the characteristics of those natural processes that self-organize, evolve, and adapt to changes in their environment. Thus, if social systems are complex, the vestiges of self-organization will look like a conspiracy. The links are there, but there is no planner, no mastermind behind the structure. What look like patterns are merely the shadows of complexity.

In the early twentieth century, a group of economists in Austria postulated a social system with characteristics similar to those of the process now described by complexity theory. The system was to consist of individuals who, while working in their own self-interest, would also cooperate because of overlapping goals and knowledge. Ultimately, this group of people would self-organize into a *free market system*. The Austrian economists followed a nonmathematical path because the processes they were describing could not be modeled by the mathematics available at the time.

The math is now available, and because the sciences of complexity can be applied directly to the Austrian school, we are better able to understand the workings of a free market. In particular, we can achieve a deeper understanding of uncertainty's role in a free market economy as well as in a free society. Uncertainty is not necessarily bad or synonymous with risk. Complex systems use uncertainty to their advantage as they adapt to changes in their environment and learn to be resilient to unexpected shocks. Uncertainty then, rather than being the source of so many problems, becomes a necessary element if a market and a society are to remain free.

This role of uncertainty is not widely understood, especially in the emerging markets. With the global economy going through yet another crisis, there is a danger that the emerging markets, which have just recently begun to operate as free market economies, will retrench due to bad times. They are not prepared for the uncertainty that is necessary if a free market is to function and to search for solutions to its economic

problems. Instead, they will tend to "restore order" by imposing a more rigid structure on their society. By doing so, they
risk losing the very elements that make a free market so desir-
able. That is not to say that nothing should be done ("Let the
free market decide!"). Rather, actions should be taken to set
limits on what individuals can do, without dictating exactly
what they should do. We will examine this seemingly contradictory statement in great detail.

This book is about the links between the Austrian school of
economics and complexity theory; however, it is nonmathematical. The intent is to draw attention to the dangers of too much
planning at either the individual or the government level. We
will find that rules are important for creating and maintaining
complexity, but the rules should be limitations, not commands.
They should encourage cooperation and ensure that the environment also encourages competition.

This book is also about the nature of uncertainty, and why it
is necessary for a free society. We often consider uncertainty to
be undesirable because it means that things are risky. We will
find that, at times, particularly when dealing with competition,
risk can only be lowered when uncertainty is *increased*. The
ability to adapt and evolve may be destroyed by reducing uncertainty. The emerging market governments are on the verge of
doing just that; they are confusing uncertainty with risk. A large
part of our discussion is tied to distinguishing between these
two similar but different states.

Peter Bernstein, in his excellent book *Against the Gods:
The Remarkable Story of Risk,* touched on this distinction. Understanding the true nature of uncertainty, he said, makes us
"free souls" who can make decisions that are useful. As he puts
it: ". . . the world of pure probability . . . has nothing to do
with . . . creative human beings struggling to find their way out
of the darkness." A large part of my effort in this work is to

help people understand the distinction between risk and uncertainty so that "risk reduction" does not destroy the freedom we cherish so much.

Because of the wide range of material, the book is divided into two parts. Part One largely deals with complexity theory and the nature of uncertainty. Apart from brief references, the major discussion of economics is deferred to Part Two, where we discuss the Austrian school of economics and its links to complexity theory. The book closes with a review of the implications that these observations have for the future of free markets. The tone is informal because I would like this book to be read by anyone who makes decisions under conditions of *true* uncertainty. We experience true uncertainty when we do not know the probabilities of the possible outcomes because we do not even know what all of the possible outcomes are. By understanding how truly ignorant we are, we will be able to make better decisions, even as we continue to make mistakes.

EDGAR E. PETERS

Concord, Massachusetts
March 1999

Acknowledgments

F irst, I would like to thank my editor, Mina Samuels, for her help and encouragement while preparing this book. I would also like to thank my colleagues at PanAgora Asset Management: Peter Rathjens, Bruce Clarke, Jarrod Wilcox, Roland Lochoff, Bill Zink, Rick Wilk, John Capeci, Georgeanne Nicozisin, Orville Yearwood, and Dave Liddell for their help and insight. Thanks also to Kalvin Kallagher for his excellent cartoons. Finally, I would like to thank my family—Sheryl, Ian, and Lucia— for once again indulging me in my need to write. Special thanks to Ian, for the David Bowie quote.

E.E.P

Contents

PART TWO

Free Markets and the Need for Uncertainty

Patterns in the Dark

CHAPTER 1

Introduction: Life, Risk, and Uncertainty

We demand rigidly defined areas of doubt and uncertainty!
—*Vroomfondel*, Hitchhiker's Guide to the Galaxy

LIFE is uncertain. We can be certain of that. Every day, we are faced with unpredictable events. Some are large. Most are small. Uncertainty makes us uneasy, nervous about the future. Uncertainty is bad. We spend time preparing for uncertainty so we are not "blindsided" or "caught off guard."

Humans have long tried to ease uncertainty by predicting the future. Early predictions were attempted through supernatural means. More recently, scientific methods have been used. Science has helped, but because some uncertainty always remains, supernatural means continue to be used, even though most of us know that they are not valid. Horoscopes, for instance, are still published in the newspapers and are widely consulted. We have a deep wish, a deep need to increase the predictability, the order of our lives. We continue to search for ways to reduce uncertainty—and the risk that we perceive accompanying it.

Yet, we know that risk taking is the only way to achieve success. The most profitable routes, both personally and professionally, are usually the risky ones. Heroes, whether they are soldiers, explorers, scientists, artists, or writers, are people who take advantage of those opportunities. By taking risks, great battles are won—in war, in the university, and in the marketplace. Risk taking advances our culture, our knowledge, and our wealth. Risk taking also breeds innovation and growth.

Here, we reach the paradox of risk and uncertainty. On the one hand, risk is something to be minimized—or even eliminated if possible. At the same time, taking a risk, or using uncertainty to our advantage, brings opportunity and advancement. Risk and uncertainty are synonymous, yet both can be good or bad. We fear risk and uncertainty, even as we know we need them.

In the dark, there is no order, only hope of
order in the midst of uncertainty.

Part of the problem is a perception that uncertainty and risk are synonymous. Are they? Risk is tied to the possibility of loss, like gambling. Uncertainty, on the other hand, is merely the unknown; loss is not always involved. Yet, uncertainty makes us more uneasy than when we face a situation that has known risks. This anxiety is bred into us. If you sit in a room in your own house, in the dark, you will feel uneasy. Despite the fact that you know all of the objects in the room and where they are placed, you imagine that other things are in those objects. They become vague shapes, patterns in the dark. We need to face this anxiety and accept intellectually that there is nothing to be afraid of. The uncertainty we face in the dark has no real risk, just perceived risk, because we do not know, for sure, what's out there. We desire an order, or perfect knowledge, that comes only when we turn on the lights. In the dark, there is no order. There is only the hope of order in the midst of uncertainty. In real life, of course, we are always "sitting in the dark," trying to guess at how things would look if we could "turn on the lights." We try to impose this order, even if there is no proof that order exists. We need order even as we extol risk taking.

So, we are torn between these two needs: the need for order, and the need for uncertainty. The urge to bring order and safety usually wins out. Yet, we need uncertainty; without it, we become stagnant and unmotivated. Leninist Communism is one example of how too much order, too much control, took the life out of a system, which then lost its ability to innovate and adapt. The lack of competition reduced the ability of the communist economy to adapt to new conditions, and, as we all know, adaptability is the key to survivorship.

We are not only afraid of *being* in the dark, we are also suspicious of being *kept* in the dark. We often feel that the universe has a hidden order that we cannot quite comprehend. In ancient times, this order was attributed to the gods—omnipotent beings who controlled humans' fates. Greek myths in particular portrayed humans as pawns in the great games played by the gods. More recently, there are suspicions of global conspiracies. These conspiracies are cited for events that are too important to be random. We no longer describe them as "acts of God," so they must be the work of other people—people who are hiding their influence over us, covering up their involvement. They are keeping the rest of us in the dark. Among the events attributed to these people are political assassinations and UFO sightings. Examining these events in minute detail results in a long list of "coincidences" which, in the minds of the conspiracy buffs, are too numerous to be truly random. There must be a central planner who is at the hub of a sinister form of order. No one admits to the conspiracy, so there must be a cover-up. Better to think that we are all being kept in the dark by sinister forces than to admit that there is no order. Yet, as we shall see, order can erupt spontaneously, without a central planner. This spontaneous order, which evolves from complexity, is often confused with conspiracy. The fact that this spontaneous order *needs* uncertainty makes the process even more counterintuitive. This spontaneous order is the basis of the "invisible hand" described by Adam Smith. A free market economy is an evolving structure with no central planner, but it does have coordinated activity by the participants.

The spontaneous nature of free markets makes them innovative and resilient, but there is a cost. The cost of freedom is uncertainty. Only by living with uncertainty can a free society thrive. For this reason, many societies slide back into totalitarian rule. They cannot accept the responsibility of living with the uncertainty that is necessary to maintain a free market. It is easier for them to rely on the certainty of a central planner than to live with the uncertainty of a free society.

In spite of our diversity, we *are* all similar. We have global characteristics that define us as humans. Yet, in detail, each of us is unique. This global order, combined with local random-ness, minimizes the chances that we will all be susceptible to the same disease. Because humanity is robust with respect to changes in its environment, continuity is maintained. Through diversity, we increase the uncertainty regarding our genetic code and gain protection against a virus's invasion. Thus, uncertainty lowers our risk from virus.

As a social system, the stock market also has the need for uncertainty. The stock market exists to give investors a venue for trading. Investors want to make as much money as possible. However, the market, as an entity, does not have this goal. The market exists to provide liquidity, plain and simple. Therefore, it is in the market's interest to make itself as complex as possible. The end result is always the rise and fall of prices and the transfer of wealth. This creates market cycles that are closely related to the business cycle. However, each market cycle has different circumstances underlying its dynamics. In one era, technology stocks are the driving force. In another, oil prices have a similar role. Each market cycle has its own story, but the end result is always the same: rising and falling prices. Once again, we have global structure and local randomness.

Why does this structure exist? To offer opportunity to all participants, while allowing no single investor to have an advantage over the others. If the market did have a predictable structure (i.e., a "perfect" trading system exists), then someone would figure it out and accumulate all of the world's wealth. The market would cease to exist; it would die. However, if the market were completely unpredictable, no one would have incentive to participate. Again, there would be no market.

Thus, we come to the paradox of capitalism and free markets: opportunity for everyone, but the advantage to no one. Each business cycle is different in detail; that is, the underlying cause of each cycle is different. No *one* investment approach will work all of the time, at least in the short term. Many approaches will work *some* of the time. So, the market needs uncertainty if it is to offer opportunity to all investors. It also needs uncertainty to perpetuate the flow of funds between investors and to ensure its own survival. By ensuring that no specific information set drives the market every time, the market diversifies the nature of its own participants. At its heart, the stock market needs uncertainty to exist and to continue existing. Uncertainty is the market's main source of stability and innovation. It needs uncertainty to perpetuate the competitive nature that is its lifeblood.

The need for uncertainty is ubiquitous. Complex systems, both physical and social, require a high level of uncertainty *at the local level* for both stability and development. This means that, as much as we may hate the idea of living in an uncertain world, uncertainty is not only inevitable, *it is necessary*. This latter observation is particularly important in the social systems that are a part of our everyday lives. Often, laws are passed or rules are made to make life more structured and less complex. What makes a social system complex is a *loose coupling* between individual participants and an increase in the number of possible paths of development. Democratic political systems and free market economies require a loose environment to ensure competition, but they also require regulations to maintain the free nature of this competition and to ensure that the common good becomes a goal of the society. Complex systems are characterized by global structure and local randomness. The global structure maintains the strength of the whole. The local randomness creates innovation and resilience. In free market economies, competition is the source of local randomness, and regulation maintains the global structure. Thus, competition requires a high level of uncertainty, which we all experience in real time. Efforts to eliminate this uncertainty would destroy the nature of a free market economy. The complexity theory used to describe this process is relatively new, but the concepts in economics go back to the nineteenth century, to the Austrian school of economics.

This book examines the relationship between the Austrian school of economics and complexity theory. In the past ten years, we have developed a better understanding of complex systems—systems that self-organize. For complexity to exist, the right conditions must be in place. A number of independent elements will then spontaneously start cooperating and will act as a single unit. Hurricanes are a common example. The weather system organizes into an entity so coherent that we give it a name, and usually assign it a personality. For the past 100 years, the Austrian school of economics has developed the theory of *subjectivism*. The Austrians believe that individuals working in their own self-interest will spontaneously self-organize when there is an overlap in goals or knowledge. There is, in fact, a direct correspondence between many concepts developed by the Austrians and those of complexity theory. Complexity theory offers a mathematical foundation to the insights of the Austrian economists.

The integration of the two fields of study could hold important lessons about the nature of free market economies. In particular, we will see that uncertainty is necessary for free markets to exist. In fact, there is a need for uncertainty in all systems where a need for change and a need for stability coexist. Free markets need stability so that people can have faith in the strength of the economy. At the same time, free markets need to be able to grow and adapt. The primary vehicle for change in a free market is competition, which requires uncertainty in order to exist.

At a time when many totalitarian governments are converting to free market economies, it is critical that they know the role uncertainty plays in such an economy. Uncertainty is the price we pay for the benefits and opportunities generated by free markets. Because totalitarian economies offer great certainty and little opportunity, the citizens of formerly totalitarian, state-controlled economies may not be prepared to live with the uncertainty that is required. When bad times come, they will be more likely to give up, and slide back into the comfort of a structured economy.

In developed markets, understanding the connection between uncertainty and the discovery process of competition prevents the passing of laws that inadvertently restrict competition by trying to protect the citizens from the impact of uncertainty, which is often confused with risk.

Other complex systems—for example, evolution and the creative process—also have a high need for uncertainty in order to generate innovation.

In the end, we see that uncertainty is not necessarily bad. It is not something to be avoided. It is not necessarily associated with risk. There are times when we need uncertainty. We may not like uncertainty, but facing our fear of the unknown is the only way to continue growing. Otherwise, we would sit in the dark, motionless, paralyzed by an unknown risk that may not exist.

PART ONE

Uncertainty, Complexity, and Spontaneous Organization

. . . one person's actions are the other person's data.
—F.A. Hayek

CHAPTER 2

Imposing Order: Conspiracies and the Mathematics of Ignorance

He sits motionless, like a spider in the centre of its web, but that web has a thousand radiations, and he knows well every quiver of each of them. . . . Is there a crime to be done . . . the word is passed to the Professor, the matter is organized and carried out. The agent may be caught. . . . But the central power which uses the agent is never caught—never so much as suspected.

—Sherlock Holmes, *The Final Problem*

The Truth Is Out There.
Trust No One.
I Want to Believe.

—Slogans from *The X-Files*

SCENARIO: A judge who spent a lifetime trying to make the world a better place goes mad. He now believes that he is Sherlock Holmes. His madness stems from a simple observation: Every day, bad things happen to good people. Could so many tragedies be mere random events? No. They must be the result of a conspiracy. Who better to mastermind such a conspiracy

11

than the Napoleon of Crime, Professor Moriarty? Moriarty is the source of chaos in the world, a chaos that is actually a sinister form of order. Who better than Holmes, the master of pure logic, to confront such heinous behavior? Only a genius of Moriarty's caliber can mask order as random events. Only the equal genius of Holmes can see through the noise and discern the hidden pattern.

Moriarty is the source of chaos in the world, a chaos that is actually a sinister form of order.

This plot comes from a movie entitled *They Might Be Giants*, written by James Goldman. It perfectly captures our ability to impose order where there is none, and to deny structure where it actually exists. A conspiracy gives meaning to randomness, and order to chaos.

Americans have a love–hate relationship with conspiracy theories. On the one hand, the American judicial system will prosecute and distrust anyone who is knowingly caught up in a conspiracy or a cover-up (often the sequel to a conspiracy). On the other hand, the American public loves to read about and share conspiracy theories. Whole groups of people, for instance, still debate and create theories about the JFK assassination. Surely such a history-changing event could not have been the result of the random behavior of an insignificant stockroom clerk! *The X-Files* television show, Oliver Stone's film *JFK*, and the continuing interest in O. J. Simpson exemplify our national obsession with conspiracy.

We look for conspiracies to explain things that we cannot understand, or prove, or ever know for sure. We hate the idea that we can be "random victims" ourselves. We hate the idea that events can happen that are beyond our individual or collective control. We hate any situation that leaves us forever ignorant of the facts. The uncertainty in such a situation requires an explanation. If we have none, we make one up. Better to think we are being kept in the dark by others than to accept that we are all in the dark. Fox Mulder, the FBI agent on *The X-Files,* has a sign on his bulletin board that says, *I Want to Believe.* What better phrase to represent our times?

Uncertainty leads to fear. Any unknown situation is threatening and therefore carries risk. However, the relationship between risk and true uncertainty is widely misunderstood. In statistics, risk and uncertainty have become synonymous. In our normal modes of thought, they have become synonymous for us, too.

The official record says otherwise. Dictionary definitions of risk and uncertainty point to the difference:

risk, n. Possibility of loss or injury.
uncertain, adj. 1. not certain; doubtful 2. Unsteady or hesitant; not firm. —uncertainty, n.

The definition of uncertainty says nothing about the chance of loss. It says nothing about risk. It says only that things are doubtful. Murphy's Law—that anything that can go wrong will—has a paranoid's version: "If anything *bad* can happen, it will." It is easy to imagine that if we are ignorant of the current situation, if we are uncertain as to what may happen, then something bad will happen. Uncertainty becomes a source of risk.

The relationship between risk and uncertainty is much more complex than we may think. Risk, for instance, can usually be quantified. True uncertainty cannot. The two terms are far from being synonymous. Later, we will see that we can lower risk by introducing uncertainty. In fact, in competition, there is nothing more dangerous or risky than a lack of uncertainty. Often, *we need uncertainty in order to reduce our risk of loss.*

Being able to distinguish between risk and uncertainty is an important step toward understanding the need for uncertainty. If we continue to confuse risk with uncertainty, we can make no progress toward understanding the interaction within a complex system such as the economy, which must generate uncertainty if it is to adapt, grow, and innovate. Randomness can generate order, but that order will have no *planned* purpose. No conspiracy is involved.

FOUR DILEMMAS

This section describes four dilemmas. You are to make four choices. In each situation, you will face the unknown. Each situation will be different and the very character of the unknown will be different because the source of uncertainty varies. Can you see what sets them apart?

Dilemma 1

You stand at a long, green table, balancing a pair of dice in your hands. Around you, a crowd is cheering and jeering simultaneously. You have just won three rolls in a row. You throw the dice. They turn up a three and a two. Five. Now you have to throw another five. $10,000 rests on this roll. If you throw a seven, you automatically lose. What are your chances?

When playing craps in Dilemma 1, the odds are reset with each play. The probabilities of rolling a five or a seven do not change because of your previous roll. Each throw is independent. The odds are well known. Throwing does not require skill. Winning is pure chance. The skill comes in playing the odds: knowing when to bet heavily and when to minimize your loss by betting little.

Consider the definition of *probability:* the percent of times that an event will happen if we repeat the event many times. The probability of throwing a five is four throws out of thirty-six, or about 11 percent. This means that if we throw the dice 1,000 times, we will get a five 110 times. Truly *random* events have a well-defined chance of happening. We often say that random fluctuations will "wash out over time." In essence, we are saying that after doing this over many days or years, we end up where we started from.

Dilemma 2

You are standing in a TV studio, dressed as a clown. Beside you is a smooth-talking game show host. You have just won a new refrigerator. The host is asking you to trade your refrigerator for whatever is behind one of three curtains (labeled, appropriately,

#1, #2, and #3). He tells you that behind one curtain is a new Porsche 911 Turbo worth over $100,000. You choose curtain #2 because you had two eggs for breakfast. The game show host shows you that curtain #1 hid a trip for two to Hawaii. He asks whether you want to switch to curtain #3 or keep curtain #2. What do you do?

Dilemma 2 is called the "Monte Hall dilemma" after the host of the popular 1960s game show, *Let's Make a Deal*. This dilemma has caused a great deal of debate in statistical circles. When you make your choice, the odds of picking the Porsche are one in three. Do the odds change when one of the other curtains is revealed not to hide the car? Some people say "No," and never change curtains. Some say "Yes," and always change. Some say, "Go with your gut. It's 50/50 now anyway." As you can see, the Monte Hall dilemma is much more complex than the dice throw. However, it still has an answer: *Always change.* Though there is not universal agreement, the general consensus is that the probabilities do change, but not to 50/50. The curtain you initially selected always has a one-in-three probability, because those were the conditions under which you chose it. However, when curtain #1 is eliminated, its one-in-three probability is now transferred to curtain #3. Curtain #3 now has a two-in-three probability of hiding the Porsche. So: Always change. Mathematicians have done simulations of the Monte Hall dilemma, and have found, after many repeated trials, that this reasoning holds up. You win about two-thirds of the time when you shift.

This leads to two important elements that Dilemmas 1 and 2 have in common:

1. All the possible outcomes are known in advance.
2. The conditions for both problems are well defined.

The Monte Hall dilemma is more complex than throwing dice, but we are still faced with a limited number of possible outcomes. Like the mathematicians, we can run the problem many times under the same conditions and find the probabilities of the possible outcomes. The event is repeatable. The risks are easy to assess. The uncertainty is measurable.

Dilemma 3

You are the Chief Economist at a large investment bank, Rathjens Brothers, Inc. The company invests billions of dollars in the bond market. Your job is to judge the direction of interest rates. You are holding a press conference. A reporter from The New York Times *asks: "What are the odds that the Federal Reserve Board [the Fed] will raise interest rates?" You note that the Fed's primary goal is to control inflation while promoting economic growth. If the economy grows too fast, prices begin to rise. Once prices begin rising, it's hard to stop inflation without having a recession and throwing people out of work. You note that with the economy expanding and unemployment at 4.5 percent, inflationary pressures may begin building, but they have not begun yet.*

"Yes," the reporter replies. "So what are the chances that the Fed will raise interest rates?"

How do you respond?

Dilemma 3 is different. You are predicting what another group of people is going to do. You are trying to anticipate a decision-making process before the group even begins that process. This dilemma is more complex than the Monte Hall dilemma. First, we can never be sure what information the Federal Reserve Open Market Committee is going to use to make its decisions. Second, even if we did know, we cannot be certain how the Committee will interpret that information. How do you reply?

You could say, "I don't know. It's a toss-up." A statistician would then say that you assigned a "subjective" probability of 50/50 because there are two possible outcomes. But then you would not be making the big bucks as Chief Economist at Rathjens Brothers. Most economists will throw out a number like 60 percent. Many will actually believe the number. But when an economist assigns a 60 percent probability to an event that cannot be measured, what does that say? Hold that thought until we work through Dilemma 4.

Dilemma 4

You are an artist. You've painted for a long time in a superrealist style. However, you have also long admired the spare lines of Japanese art. You would like to integrate the two styles, but you don't know how. The only way to develop a new style is to continue painting and experiment. You know that if you work at it long enough you may be able to come up with the synthesis you desire. However, you haven't a clue about how it will turn out or whether you will be successful. You look ahead and see years of trying concepts that do not work, or work only partially. While you are working out the problem, the art-buying public may not understand what you are up to. You may end up starving, or forgotten. On the other hand, you may create an entirely new school of painting. Should you follow this path?

If you follow the uncertain course in Dilemma 4, your friends, spouse, and/or parents will ask what your odds of success are. You will give them an answer: "Seventy percent that I'll succeed, but only 20 percent that I'll found a new school of painting." Where do these numbers come from? In Dilemma 4, you know even less about the future than when you were asked about interest rates in Dilemma 3. Are you just guessing?

FACING THE DILEMMAS

Dilemmas 3 and 4 are too complex to assign probabilities. We can repeatedly throw the dice in Dilemma 1, or repeat trials in Dilemma 2, but the last two dilemmas cannot be repeated under exactly the same conditions. Why? *Because we do not know what the current conditions are.* We are living in a state of *true* uncertainty. We can also use the terms *ambiguous* or *ignorant,* but no matter how we look at these two dilemmas, we do not know what is going on. We know only a part of the picture. The uncertainty we face in Dilemmas 3 and 4 is clearly different from the uncertainty of Dilemmas 1 and 2. We tend to express our decision-making processes as if we know the probabilities. Yet how often do we actually face such situations? When playing games, we face them often. In real life, hardly ever. Instinctively, we know that there is a difference between times when we know the probabilities, and times when we do not. Consciously, we rarely admit the distinction. However, if risk and uncertainty *are* different concepts, then we need to know what separates them.

As we stated earlier, risk is associated with potential loss. The loss itself is not defined. It could be the loss of money, or the loss of something less tangible, like your reputation; it could even be a failing grade on an exam. The combination of words— *potential loss*—confuses people. Risky situations are uncertain, but are uncertain situations risky? Sometimes, yes; sometimes, no. All four dilemmas have uncertain outcomes, but only Dilemmas 1 and 2 involve real losses. Dilemmas 3 and 4 do not even have right answers, let alone a potential loss. The uncertainty comes from the fact that we do not know all of the possible outcomes. It is therefore impossible to calculate the probability of occurrence. A probability is how often a potential outcome occurs when the event is repeated many times. We can know how often a five shows up in 1,000 rolls of a pair of dice. We cannot know how often we will succeed in creating a new style of painting.

Meanwhile, where did the probabilities in Dilemmas 3 and 4 come from? Are we just pulling them out of the air? Some would say yes. Some would say that we are setting subjective probabilities, though how we do so is unknown. Behavioral psychologists think that we are comparing what we know of the current situation with past situations. As the economist in Dilemma 3, if you see that the current conditions are 60 percent similar to other times when the Fed has raised interest rates, you will say that the probability is 60 percent, though that is not what you really mean. You are not saying that if we repeated current conditions 1,000 times, the Fed would raise rates 60 percent of the time. Instead, you are basing your statement on the similarity with the past. Your answer has nothing to do with odds at all. Behavioral psychologists have found that, when faced with incomplete information, we often base our decision on similarity with past experience. Probability does not even come into it. How can we know probabilities if we have incomplete information?

MORE INFORMATION?

Do we then conclude that all we need is more information? In many cases, that is true. However, when faced with competition, that may not be true.

Lord Keynes had his beauty contest. Richard Thaler, in his book, *The Winner's Curse,* performs an interesting variation on it. Suppose you have a crowd of people gathered in a room. You tell them that they are all to write down a number between 1 and 100. The person who gets closest to the average of all the submitted numbers will win a prize. What number would you guess?

There are three general strategies. One group of people will probably decide, "I don't know what everyone else will do. It's probably random, so I'll guess 50."

The second group will think, "This group looks pretty dumb. They'll probably all guess 50. So I'll guess 25 and bring down the average."

The third group will think, "This group looks smart. They'll probably guess 25, so I'll guess 12."

Thaler has performed this experiment many times. Generally, the average is 12 to 15.

However, suppose we take Thaler's experiment a little further. We tell everyone at the start that the winning answer is usually 12, and explain why. What happens then? The same thing, except now 3 becomes the winning guess because everyone is now basing the guess on 12 instead of 50. However, someone may decide that now that everyone else understands how 12 was the answer, they will all answer 3, so he'll answer 6 and bring up the average. If others guess the same, then the winning answer will change yet again. If the game is continued, there will be no stable answer. The competition ensures that the system never settles down to a stable equilibrium value. It keeps changing as each participant tries to outguess the others. In this case, additional information—explaining the workings of the game in the first round—succeeded only in increasing uncertainty, not decreasing it.

This type of game can be extrapolated to many real-life situations. It can be used to model everything from price wars to stock market trading and arms races. It shows that, when faced with competition, more information does not necessarily reduce uncertainty. It may even increase it.

Thaler's game can still be equated with risk. There is something at stake here. However, true uncertainty is merely the unknown. Potential loss does not have to be involved. If risky situations are uncertain, why do we also think that uncertain situations are risky? If $a = b$, does not $b = a$? This latter statement, the Communicative Law of basic algebra, is not universal. Sometimes $b \neq a$, as we shall see.

THE ELLSBERG PARADOX

Dr. Daniel Ellsberg (of Pentagon Papers fame) published, in 1961, a study that highlighted the difference between uncertainty and risk, as well as how we prefer known probabilities to the ambiguity of the unknown. "Subjective probability," beloved by Bayesian mathematicians, is not used by real people.

In the Ellsberg Paradox, you are shown an urn that contains 90 balls. Of these, 30 are red, and the remaining 60 are an unknown mixture of black and yellow balls. One ball is to be drawn from the urn, and you are to be paid an amount of money if a particular color ball is chosen. You are given two payoff options to choose from:

	Red	**Black**	**Yellow**
Option 1	$100	$ 0	$ 0
Option 2	$ 0	$100	$ 0

Look over Options 1 and 2. Decide which you would choose.

Ellsberg then offers you two other options. The drawing will be from the same urn, with the same mixture of red, black, and yellow balls as before:

	Red	Black	Yellow
Option 3	$100	$ 0	$100
Option 4	$ 0	$100	$100

Which of these two options would you choose? Be honest!

Most people choose Option 1 for the first payoff, and Option 4 for the second. Why? In Option 1, you know that you have a one-in-three chance of winning. You have no idea of the chance of winning in Option 2. It could be higher than one-in-three, or it could be zero. Better to go with the odds you know.

Option 4 is chosen for much the same reason. You know that Option 4 has a two-in-three probability because 60 of the 90 balls are either yellow or black, but you do not know the odds of finding a red *or* a yellow ball. Again, better to go with the odds you know.

Alone, each choice appears rational. Remember, though, you chose *both* Options 1 and 4. Here is where the "paradox" comes in. If you are using subjective probability to make your choice, choosing Option 1 over Option 2 would mean that you believe that a red ball is more likely to be drawn than a black ball. However, choosing Option 4 over Option 3 implies a belief that "black or yellow" is more likely than "red or yellow." Black is thus more likely than red when choosing Option 4. Choosing both Option 4 *and* Option 1 under the same conditions is irrational, according to the tenets of subjective probability.

Why do the majority of people choose Options 1 and 4? Because when faced with the unknown, or *true uncertainty,* we are more comfortable with what we know than what we don't know. Uncertainty is different from risk. Uncertainty is more dangerous than low-but-known odds. Uncertainty is ignorance. We hate being ignorant.

Reducing Risk with Uncertainty

Not only are risk and uncertainty not equivalent, it is even possible to lower risk by introducing uncertainty into a situation. In competition, being predictable puts you at a disadvantage. Reducing predictability, by increasing uncertainty, can lower your risk. The following two examples are taken from Ivar Ekeland's excellent book, *The Broken Dice*. My slant on them will be slightly different.

Ekeland describes the goalie's dilemma in soccer. In a penalty kick, one opposing player gets an opportunity to boot the ball into the goal, which is protected only by the goalie. The goalie cannot move before the ball is kicked. However, if he delays moving left or right until after the ball is kicked, he will surely miss. So, he must move simultaneously with the kick, and anticipate which way the kicker will boot the ball. The player has obviously studied the goalie's past defenses. If the goalie has a tendency to move right, he kicks left. The goalie cannot have a tendency to move one way or the other. His best strategy is to randomly move right or left 50 percent of the time. At worst, he will stop half of the goal kicks. At best—well, there *are* lucky runs, even in soccer. The goalie, in increasing the uncertainty level of the game by making himself less predictable, has *lowered* his risk. On the other hand, any predictable behavior by either player will result in less uncertainty but higher risk.

Usually we want a better payoff than 50/50 to play the game. Ekeland gives another example of how we can actually increase our expected return by increasing uncertainty. The game is a simplified version of poker. The players are you and a dealer. First, you each bet a dollar. The dealer takes a regular deck of 52 playing cards, removes all the sevens, and places them face up in front of her. She then shuffles the remaining cards and deals you one card, face down. You look at your card. If the card is greater than seven, you win. (An ace counts as "one.") You have a 50 percent chance of winning. The dealer has all of the sevens. There are 24 cards greater than seven (eights through Kings in four suits), and 24 cards below seven, giving you 50/50 odds. Upon receiving your card and looking at it, you can do one of three things:

1. You can fold, and lose your dollar.
2. You can call.
3. You can up the ante another dollar.

If you choose the latter action, the dealer can do one of two things:

1. Fold, and lose a dollar.
2. Call, and bet $2.

If your card is greater than seven, you now win $2. Simple.

As the player, you may want to set up a strategy, or "system." There are four potential systems:

1. Always fold.
2. Always up the ante.
3. Up the ante on a good card, fold on a bad card.
4. Fold on a good card, up the ante on a bad card.

Strategy 1 is silly. You always lose, so we can dispense with that system right away. Strategy 4 holds little promise as well.

Once the dealer begins calling, you do not have a prayer. You always lose $2. Strategy 2 is interesting, but if the dealer calls every time, you end up back at even; you win half of the time. That's no fun. Strategy 3 seems to be the most sensible. Increase the ante when you are sure of winning, fold when you might lose. The dealer will eventually realize that she cannot win when you up the ante, and will begin folding. Again, you are back to breaking even. Your expected gain is $0.

In each case, the *best* you can do is break even Why? Because your "system" is predictable. In the parlance of the stock market, any inefficiency you have found can be "arbitraged" away; that is, any advantage can be systematically discovered and eliminated by the competition. Is there any way to make a strategy less predictable?

Yes. The problem with the *systematic* strategies outlined above is that they are easily predictable. A winning strategy is a combination of Strategies 3 and 4: *Up the ante on a good card, but also up the ante on a bad card one-third of the time.*

The strategy of upping the ante on a bad card has a name. It is called *bluffing.* By bluffing one-third of the time, you have reduced the predictability of your actions. The dealer, knowing that you often bluff on a bad card, will try to guess which action you are taking. However, she cannot guess, because you are doing it at random. Your system cannot be arbitraged away. Your expected gain has gone from zero to 35 cents for every dollar bet—a considerable return.

You must be completely *random* in your bluffing. If you bluff every third card, or in runs, the dealer will discern this pattern of behavior. Bluffing must be randomly dispersed, but must occur on one-third of the bad cards for this system to work. It is also imperative that you be *caught* bluffing. The occasional loss only succeeds in confusing your opponent more.

By contrast, the systematic approach actually increases your risk of loss because of its predictability. Each strategy has low uncertainty and high risk. Even after repeated play, the best you can hope for is to break even.

Bluffing, by adding uncertainty through randomness to your behavior, has increased your return and reduced your risk. Again, uncertainty and risk are not synonymous. In this case, uncertainty works to your advantage.

The strategy also illustrates the universal characteristics of complex adaptive systems: local randomness and global structure. In this case, the local randomness is the bluff itself. The global structure is statistical. Your expected profit is 35 cents, given enough hands in the set you measure. No matter how many sets of hands you play, your profit will always be 35 cents per hand. The exact path you take to reach this global average will be different with each set, but the end result will be the same.

ORDER WITHOUT PLAN

Here we come to the crux of the matter. We began this chapter by talking about conspiracy theories, the attempt to impose order on random events. The essence of conspiracy theories lies in the belief that seemingly unrelated events must be related because there is a plan, a hidden order, behind the chaos. Because there is a plan, there must be a planner. (*"I Want to Believe."*) In other words, the relationship behind the events must be part of a grand design. Professor Moriarty and his master plan lurk behind each seemingly random event. Yet, we have already seen that a combination of randomness and order can, in fact, exist. In the case of simple poker, a profit will always result (after a sufficient number of hands) without cheating. It is, as biologist Stuart Kauffman would say, order for free. No planning is necessary to create this kind of order.

It is all well and good to find statistical order, but what about *causal* order? In the next chapters we will examine complex systems in which order really does arise spontaneously, and for free, in real life. While not completely statistical, this order does still, paradoxically, depend on stochastic elements for its character. Order still needs randomness to exist. Moriarty plans with dice.

CHAPTER 3

Uncertainty, Vagueness, and Ambiguity: The Need for Information

Is knowledge knowable? If not, how do we know this?
—Woody Allen

When there is shouting, there is no true knowledge.
—Leonardo da Vinci

EVER notice how things never change, but are still always different? For most of us, completely "new" experiences are rare. We usually go through the same routines every day, and we like having that structure. We like the reliability of going to work at the same time and meeting with the same people. But we would be bored if every day were exactly like every other. Within our daily routine, we like *some* variety, but not too much. If each day were completely different, we would feel lost and unsure of ourselves. Our natural tendency is to try to balance regularity and novelty. This tendency, which often shows up in nature, ensures that we are constantly faced with ambiguous situations. We consider some of these ambiguous situations risky, but we saw in Chapter 2 that uncertainty can reduce our risk and generate opportunity. This opportunity can be generated in situations we face again and again.

A common example occurs when we buy a new car. We go to a dealer and look at the cars in showroom. We test-drive a car and negotiate the price with a salesperson. Those are the *typical* activities involved in buying a car. However, each time we go into a negotiation, the details are different. The typical conditions for this transaction are stored in our memory, based on our experience in the past. However, strategies that were successful in the past may not work this time. Suppose that when the previous negotiating was done, the economy was poor and new-car sales were slow. We felt that we had an advantage because the dealer had rows of cars on the lot, so we were tough negotiators. This time, however, the economy is booming. Car sales are brisk, and there is a waiting list for the model of car we want. How do we relate our past experience to the current situation?

VAGUENESS AND AMBIGUITY

We can divide uncertainty into two broad types: vagueness and ambiguity. Vagueness refers to an inability to precisely define something by establishing a definite cutoff for classification purposes. "Short," for instance, is a vague concept. When are people short? When their height is 5 feet, 2 inches? Is someone who is 5 feet, 2.5 inches no longer short? The concept of "short" cannot be precisely defined. It is *vague*.

In contrast, the uncertainty involved in buying a new car is characterized by *ambiguity*. The situation is similar to others we have faced in the past. There are *degrees* of similarity, but there are also substantial differences. We are trying to match a specific situation in the past, and the action we took then, with an ongoing situation in the present. The similarities and differences will influence our decisions.

Ambiguity occurs when the *choice* between two or more objects or actions is unclear. We lack sufficient information about the possible outcome of our actions. Our decisions are made under conditions of ambiguity. An earlier example centered on whether the Fed will raise interest rates. Usually, a set of "ideal" conditions allows us to know with certainty whether the Fed will raise the rates. However, because history does not repeat itself exactly, we never experience those conditions unambiguously. *Some* of the expected criteria are present, and our conclusion has to be based on the preponderance of evidence. The situation is ambiguous. More information may help, but, as we saw in Chapter 2, under conditions of competition, more information may increase the uncertainty. In addition, because our potential store of knowledge cannot cover *all* of the possible outcomes, we will always operate under ambiguous circumstances. We refer to this ambiguity as uncertainty.

Vagueness, although an interesting subject all in itself, is not what we are discussing. Vague concepts are not related to the passage of time or to a dynamic process. "Short" is a state (often, of mind) that is vague. We are examining the need for uncertainty in complex systems that evolve and change in real time. As such, we are really talking about ambiguity.

There are three basic levels of ambiguity. They stem from (1) whether we have sufficient details, (2) whether confusion is present, and (3) whether conflicting evidence clouds the outcome. They characterize how we approach our problems. One way of dealing with uncertainty is to make sure that we are defining the problem in the best manner, given the information we have. How much reliable knowledge do we have? How much more would be helpful? Let's examine each type of ambiguity.

"COULD YOU BE MORE SPECIFIC?"

Often, the problem or the object under investigation is not defined with enough precision. We classify a situation so broadly that it could fit one of many possibilities. Suppose we describe a friend as "male." That narrows the image a little, but there are still many categories that our male person can fit into. The ambiguity comes from not being specific enough in our description or classification. This ambiguity is a source of uncertainty.

In the movie *Fargo*, the detective, Marge, asks a local girl to describe a suspect. The girl can only describe him as "funny looking."

"Could you be more specific?" Marge asks.

"He was just funny looking," the girl replies.

"Funny looking" could mean any combination of things. The man could have a wart on his nose. He could have reminded the girl of Bozo the Clown. He could have had big feet. Her description is ambiguous. The situation would appear to become less ambiguous if the suspect were described as a short man with dark curly hair. However, the girl did not use those words because "funny looking" was a qualitative rather than a specific physical description. She was describing the man's attitude, and the look in his eye. If you have seen the movie, you know that the girl's description was, in fact, accurate. The phrase "funny looking" was interpreted by Marge and the audience as a physical description, when it was actually a description of the man's character. Even as a qualitative description, the term could be taken many ways, and that was the source of its ambiguity and uncertainty.

When the evidence or description is not specific enough, we face another level of uncertainty. Only knowledge can help us make the situation less ambiguous.

CONFUSION

Confusion can cause uncertainty. That statement seems obvious, but what is the difference between confusion and conflicting opinions? Confusion occurs when we identify one situation as another. The evidence supports both answers, but only one is right. Conflicting opinions occur where there is no right answer. People commonly interchange confusion and conflicting opinions. Recognizing the difference between the two leads to resolution by argument or resolution by compromise. In a case of conflicting opinion, compromise is the only rational solution because there is no "right" answer. Where confusion is present, one side should be able to sway the other side by using the right evidence and logic.

Confusing evidence indicates that an event under study has more than one explanation, but the explanations do not really overlap. However, there is only one answer. Take the Ptolemaic model of the universe. The ancient Greeks observed that the sun, moon, stars, and planets (or "wandering stars") travel across the sky every day, so they assumed the universe revolved around the Earth. This explanation agreed with their theological conceptions that the Earth (and humankind) was at the center of the universe. Aristotle, for instance, thought that objects fell to the Earth because of their desire to be at the center of the universe. In the second century, Ptolemy combined the cosmology of the ancient Greeks with his own observations. The model he created fit all of the facts. Ptolemy could even adjust the model for the fact that the wandering stars (the planets) did not always go across the sky, but sometimes reversed course. However, as we now know, his model was wrong. The ancients were confused about many things. First, they misunderstood the nature of outer space, which they generally assumed was

water. Second, they assumed that our planet was the focus of
the creator, and therefore of the universe. Finally, because ce-
lestial bodies were going across the sky, they assumed they must
be circling Earth. It was, after all, the simplest explanation. In
the sixteenth century, Copernicus theorized that the solar system revolved around the Sun, a model that ancient Greeks had
suggested in the third century B.C. When Copernicus unveiled
his model in 1543, there was a good deal of uncertainty over the
nature of the universe. Both models, the Ptolemaic and the
Copernican, fit the facts, but only one could be right. The uncertainty existed because the ancients had a confused interpretation of the evidence. Later, more information cleared up the
confusion and eliminated the uncertainty. That information
came from Galileo, whose work with the telescope gave the un-
ambiguous evidence that we now accept.

*The Ptolemaic model of the universe was
wrong, even if it fit the facts.*

Confusion, a temporary form of uncertainty, can be cleared up with increased knowledge.

Conflicting Evidence

Sharp disagreement in claims or beliefs ranks high among the regular occurrences of uncertainty in society. Often, there are situations where evidence supports more than one way of viewing a problem. However, the differing viewpoints, although based on similar evidence, lead to very different conclusions. This confusion can often, but not always, be resolved with further evidence. Knowledge is not wisdom, and some situations call for wisdom rather than facts.

In the realm of science, we can resolve most conflicting opinions with facts, as in the Ptolemaic and Copernican views of the universe. Such controversies continue. An example is the theory of cold dark matter. Dark matter is postulated for one reason: Current theory would be seriously wrong without it. In the past 50 years, scientists have been able to estimate, with a fair degree of accuracy, the total mass of the universe. Current theory also states that gravitation comes from the attraction of large masses. However, if we measure the current mass of the universe (based on observed mass), something is missing. There is not enough mass to hold galaxies together. In fact, there is not nearly enough. The measurable part of the universe reveals a mass 200 billion times the mass of our Sun. However, for there to be enough mass for the universe to hold together, 1 trillion times the mass of our Sun is needed. So, either matter exists that we cannot see, or the entire theory of the universe is wrong. Needless to say, most scientists are holding the former thought and have postulated that the universe is full of matter that is cold and dark, so we cannot see it or sense its presence by measuring radiation (hence the "cold" part of the description). Other scientists reject this theory as a "plug." It conveniently endorses the current theory (retaining all the work that scientists have done) but postulates something that cannot be seen or measured. A lot of uncertainty now surrounds the nature of the universe. An easy resolution would be the discovery of cold and dark matter, but until that happens, the uncertainty remains. The implications are profound. If there is no dark matter, then the entire atomic theory is seriously flawed, as is the big bang theory of the creation of the universe. Our whole conception of nature would change. We know something is wrong, but the explanations are ambiguous. The one you choose depends on your point of view. The uncertainty could only be resolved by a discovery of natural law.

In economics, the situation is worse. To some observers, a strong economy is good news. More production, low unemployment, and a happy populace result from a strong economy. To others, a strong economy means the onset of inflation, high interest rates, and a deteriorating standard of living. The future is uncertain because the information we have is ambiguous. It could mean either the beginning of a golden age, or the beginning of the end of the current business cycle. To predict the future, investors and economists pore over economic information, but they give us multiple interpretations. Job creation can be down, which means that the economy is slowing. However, the job creation number is actually the number of new people on the work rolls. What if the reason job creation is down is because there are not enough qualified people to fill the open positions? Then a lower-than-expected number of new jobs created is actually a sign of an employment crunch and a strong economy. Once again, the information only adds to our uncertainty because the situation is ambiguous; it can be interpreted in more than one way. In economics, however, the meaning of conflicting information is resolved with the passage of time. Eventually, the predicted event either does or does not come true. There *is* resolution, but only at that stage of the cycle. The problem then becomes: What comes next? In science, the discovery of a natural law may come tomorrow, or it may come in 50 years. The time to resolution does not depend on our efforts to understand. In economics, there is a definitive answer, but by the time we receive it, it is too late.

IS KNOWLEDGE KNOWABLE?

We have seen that there are three types of ambiguity:

1. Nonspecificity of the evidence.
2. Confusion in the evidence.
3. Conflicting evidence.

In each case, increasing knowledge may decrease ambiguity and thereby reduce uncertainty. Sometimes, uncertainty is reduced but not eliminated. In other instances, more information does not reduce uncertainty. In particular, a true case of conflict is not resolvable by more evidence if ideology is a part of the conflict.

In some situations, ambiguity cannot be reduced. There are no "correct" ways to resolve the ambiguity, and the information flow is time-dependent. Most economic scenarios fit this description. In the next chapter, we will see how important the *flow* of time is in understanding the importance of uncertainty.

CHAPTER 4

Complexity and Time: The Dynamics of Uncertainty

There is no present, just the near past and the immediate future.
—George Carlin

Everything is simpler than you think and at the same time more complex than you imagine.
—Johann Wolfgang von Goethe

PREVIOUSLY, I characterized uncertainty as "merely the unknown." Many readers will undoubtedly take exception to that definition, and well they should. Defining uncertainty as an unknown future implies that the future is fixed, and merely needs to be discovered and accurately predicted. This is nonsense. I may as well say that the world works like *Let's Make a Deal*. In the Monte Hall dilemma, we had to predict which curtain was hiding the Porsche 911 Turbo. The actual location had already been determined. We had to find it by trying to understand the workings of the *Let's Make a Deal* gang. Many people look at their own future this way. They believe that the actual circumstances of what we are and what we will be have already been set. Every day, we *appear* to be faced with choices. Unlike textbook cases, real choices are filled with ambiguity because of our ignorance of the relevant facts. Still, our task is to make "the right decision." The correctness of our decisions will be determined in time, but there is always a right choice. (Only one curtain hides a Porsche; the others conceal lesser prizes.) In truth, however, even if there were a right decision, we would never know for sure which of the many actions we could have taken was the right one. The right choice may have been one that we were not even aware of. If we are not aware of all the possible choices, how can we know whether we have made the right choice? Even time will not tell.

In this context, it is easy to see that our conception of time shapes our perception of uncertainty. Uncertainty and time are inseparable, although we often wish that this were not so. We like to think of time as a river, always flowing in one direction. This image offers us the possibility of stepping out of the river onto dry land. Then we would have the ability to walk back upstream to experience or change past events, or to go forward and see what lies ahead. Classic science fiction, beginning with H.G. Wells's *The Time Machine*, has dealt with this concept for over a century. It has been reinforced by Einstein's General Theory of Relativity, which popular literature has borrowed to characterize time as "the fourth dimension." A dimension can be moved around in. Conceiving time as a physical entity, or as a fixed set of events, makes uncertainty less threatening. We may be ignorant of the future, but time still has a structure. We are merely too limited to perceive it. However, if the future is fixed in this manner, why do we feel uncertain? Uncertainty would not be a problem if the future were fixed, but unknown.

If that were so, there would be no free will, and the future, like the Porsche behind the curtain, would be merely hidden.

If uncertainty is not as simple as an unknown future, what is it? What does it have to do with time? Real time, uncertainty, and complexity are linked together. Only through reevaluating our conception of time can we hope to understand the nature of uncertainty. This relates to all complex systems, but we confine ourselves here to considering "time" as we experience it. We shall see that time and complexity intrinsically generate uncertainty. Because we cannot stop time, the only way to eliminate uncertainty is to reduce complexity. Reducing complexity reduces freedom. However, before we get to issues of complexity, we must examine time.

REAL TIME

Real time is change. Real time does not flow, it *is* flow. Time is a process, not a state. As events transpire, our universe changes, and time moves forward. If there were no change, there would be no time. We live in the present, but the present is fleeting. As George Carlin says, the present does not exist because as soon as we are aware of the present, it is already the past, and the future is the present.

We make decisions in the ever changing present. Economist G.F.S. Shackle called the present "the moment-in-being." Our memory defines the moment-in-being by the events leading up to the moment, and by our anticipation or expectation of what will happen afterward. However, the human mind cannot anticipate all of the possible consequences of any course of action. If such anticipation were possible, we would calculate and base our decisions on traditional probabilities. Probabilities are determined by the number of potential consequences, and by finding their frequency, or how often they occur. By definition, probabilities must add to 1, or account for 100 percent of the possibilities. We might then list the possibilities and how frequently they occur—an activity not unlike rolling the dice in Chapter 2. A five can occur if we roll 3-2, 2-3, 4-1, or 1-4. These are the four different combinations of the two dice that can yield a five. There are 36 possible combinations of the face of the dice, so a five has a 4-in-36 (approximately 11 percent) chance of happening. A two, on the other hand, can only occur through a 1-1 roll, which has a 1-in-36 (2 percent) chance of happening.

Wouldn't it be nice if every time we made a decision, we could see all of the possible outcomes? This rarely happens. For instance, when we make a career change, we can only dimly see where the future can take us. Important decisions usually have so many possible consequences that we cannot know them all. Our inability to see all of the possible outcomes limits our understanding of the scope of a problem, and uncertainty is generated. Uncertainty is usually amplified if, as is usually the case, the action being undertaken can be tried only once. In addition, the consequences of our actions are complex. What we do influences many things beyond our immediate surroundings. In our chosen professions, we can touch and affect many lives both positively and negatively. The impact of our decisions will always go beyond our own awareness.

This leads to another aspect of uncertainty in real time that is rarely considered: *surprise*. Because we cannot know all of the possible outcomes, unexpected events do occur. Often, they result from the actions of others, many of whom are probably not aware of their impact on our decisions or our lives.

A personal anecdote illustrates this point. My undergraduate degree is in mathematics. My first job when I finished college was as an underwriter for an insurance company in Newark,

New Jersey. In 1975, when I was 23 years old, my wife and I decided that we should really learn something about investing, to prepare for the time when we might actually have some money to invest. I went to the Newark Public Library (a very fine library, by the way) and browsed among the investment stacks. Sandwiched in with the usual "How to Make a Million in the Stock Market" variations was the first edition of Burton Malkiel's, *A Random Walk Down Wall Street*. I had no idea who Burton Malkiel was, but the book seemed to be well written. I took it home and was startled to discover that mathematics could be applied to investing. This was an epiphany. Here was a field in which I could apply math (which I loved), have fun, and even make a good living. I signed up in the MBA program at Rutgers Graduate School of Management. After a couple of years, I found myself in the field of quantitative investment management, a field that I have now worked in for over 20 years.

Consider the sequence of events here. First came the decision to learn something about investing, for future use. I sought out a novelty, with a purpose in mind. Next came the surprise of learning that my math background could introduce an entirely different future. My complete change of career and my decision to learn something about investing changed my life and my family's life. My career and my own contributions to the field of investing are unexpected consequences of Dr. Malkiel's decision to write a book about random walk theory. Dr. Malkiel, of course, is completely unaware of the way he changed my life— and indirectly affected many other readers. Novelty, surprise, and unexpected consequences are the properties of real time.

The fact that novelty occurs because we cannot anticipate all of the consequences of our actions means that uncertainty is a natural part of life in general. It cannot be eliminated no matter how hard we try. As life flows forward in real time, novel situations, unanticipated by our limited perspective, continually arise. The test of our resolve and the resilience of the choices we have made are dependent on how we handle these unexpected events. Here is where we encounter the sciences of complexity. Complex systems are able both to generate novelty and to absorb novelty as innovation. Many of the topics we have discussed so far have been taken from Austrian economics and philosophy. They have been qualitative discussions, often specific to their respective fields. What we need is a general theory of uncertainty: why it exists, and why it is necessary. We also need to quantify the concepts so that we have a general approach to, or a model of, uncertainty. Complexity theory does just that.

COMPLEXITY

There is an order lurking behind many seemingly random events. It is not an order brought about by conscious planning, but we can often sense its presence. Because we do not understand it, we assume that it is being purposely hidden from us. Moriarty is keeping us in the dark. This form of order comes from complexity. In a complex system, order arises spontaneously even though the individual elements are not directly connected and there is no overall planner. This spontaneous, unplanned order has many names in many fields. In meteorology, it can be called hurricanes, or tornadoes, or typhoons. In the study of human creativity, it is called inspiration. In investment analysis, we refer to "bull" and "bear" markets. In economics, it is called "the invisible hand." All these terms refer to the ability of seemingly random elements to spontaneously organize into a coherent structure. The evidences of this ability have been collected into one major field of study: the science of complexity.

Complex systems create something in addition to order. Paradoxically, complexity also breeds uncertainty. How can complexity generate both order *and* uncertainty? It is all a matter of scale. The order is global, a supremely large scale. Uncertainty is in the details. Think of a physical structure such as an oak tree. We can easily identify an oak tree at a glance. However, each oak tree is different. Its shape, the width and number of its branches, and the profusion of its leaves are all unique. No two oak trees are identical. Yet, we can always tell an oak tree from a pine tree. Why? Because each oak tree has a *type* of bark, a *type* of leaf, and a *typical* shape. Each of these types represents *global characteristics,* which are a function of the tree's DNA. The uncertainty lies in *unique characteristics,* which are a function of the environment. We can plant an acorn and predict with 100 percent certainty that it will grow into an oak tree (as long as it survives, of course). However, we can predict nothing about how many branches the tree will have or how tall it will grow. The details are unique. We are completely in the dark about them.

A tree is a physical artifact of a complex process. When we live within a complex process, such as a free-market economy, we can be certain of the global characteristics of our environment, while being completely uncertain about what we will face today. This uncertainty is what gives us so many opportunities. A complex process such as a free-market economy will be stable and predictable in its overall structure, but will still *need uncertainty* to maintain its stability. In economics, competition creates uncertainty as it provides the lifeblood of the system itself.

A complex system always has a function or purpose. This function is a state, not a result. The global ecosystem promotes the stable transfer of energy to maintain organic life. A free-market economy promotes the trade of goods and services among participants who seek to increase their wealth. The goal of a complex system is not a static "equilibrium." It is, instead, a dynamic and evolving state that is ever changing, ever creative, but ever stable. The details as to how it achieves this state are never constant. Because a complex system does not need a specific sequence of events to achieve its goal of a stable state, it is resilient despite unexpected changes in its environment, and it creatively adapts itself to maintain its goal. It uses uncertainty to generate order, but the "unique" features of the order it generates are not predictable. Even as a complex system turns uncertainty into order, it also generates more uncertainty.

COMPLEXITY AND RANDOMNESS

What sets a complex system apart from a random system? A random system is not unexplainable; it is merely so complicated that it is unpredictable. Rolling dice is a process we fully understand, but the interaction of the many elements involved makes it unpredictable. How is this different from a complex system such as the stock market? Aren't people just rolling dice there, too?

There are many formal differences between complex and random systems, but this book is not offering a formal study. For our purposes, the difference lies in the impact of time—real time, as discussed before. In a random system, time is of no consequence. What happens now is not dependent on the past, nor will it influence the future. Each roll of the dice is isolated in time. A complex system evolves through time. Although they are difficult to predict, complex systems do depend on the past to understand the present. Future possibilities depend on past choices. The options available to us have been largely determined by decisions we have made in the past. Although they are "path-dependent," complex systems are not "predetermined." In fact, a defining characteristic of complex systems is their ability to reach the same goal through multiple means. An acorn always grows into an oak tree, given the weather and soil conditions that allow it to survive.

Complex systems, then, have local uncertainty and global certainty. They generate change, and they are resilient to unexpected shocks. They turn uncertainty into order, and they reverse order back into uncertainty. They evolve and change through time, and they do so without a central planner. Complex systems are everywhere. In fact, real life is one huge complex system. How is such behavior possible? First, we need to understand the general class of complex systems. By understanding their nature, we will see the important role uncertainty plays in maintaining stability. When we understand natural systems, we will understand the role of uncertainty in a free society.

Because we hate living with uncertainty, we often try to make complex systems, such as the economy, more predictable and less uncertain. However, making a complex system more predictable also makes it less resilient to shocks, and less creative. Lowering uncertainty reduces complexity, often with disastrous effects. For instance, making an organization more structured may reduce its ability to innovate even as it achieves more efficiency in day-to-day operations. Creative, adaptive behavior increases with lower amounts of structure and higher levels of uncertainty. Having no structure will result in day-to-day chaos. To achieve the right balance of uncertainty and structure, we need to understand what we are dealing with. The next section deals with the actual workings of complex systems in a general form.

CHARACTERISTICS OF COMPLEXITY

Complex systems work within a balancing act. On the one hand, a complex system must be stable; it must keep working even if one piece of it breaks down or dies. On the other hand, a complex system must also change with time, adapting to competing changes in its environment. A *decentralized* structure—a system in which the parts are not aware of the whole—is the only one capable of incorporating such divergent goals. The process works through elaborate networks, or webs, where the individual elements of the system are loosely connected. For many people, the concept of complex systems breaks down at this point. We have been culturally conditioned to believe that the only *organized* system is one that has a central planner of some type. We have come to equate organization with bureaucracy. A bureaucracy is hierarchical. In business, an "organization chart" is synonymous with such a structure. An all-powerful head is represented at the top of the chart, and lesser beings feed off their connection to it. Only the head of the chart, the central authority, knows the big picture. Socialist governments were designed with this structure in mind.

In contrast, information is decentralized in complex systems. No single element knows the big picture. The knowledge of the system is spread through all of the elements. A recent, well-publicized example of such a system is the Internet, which was designed as a decentralized computer system to be used by the U.S. military. In the event of a nuclear war, the major systems in the country would be connected, but even if particular sites were destroyed, the system would still work. The Internet is really nothing more than a series of instructions that allow computers to communicate with each other. Each day, more and more computers are added to the system. The Internet makes many people uneasy because it is growing so quickly and no one is in charge of it. Innovations are occurring at a rapid pace, yet there is no central planning authority. No one knows what is going on in the system as a whole. There is no Moriarty pulling the strings in the World Wide Web. The Internet exemplifies the characteristics of a complex system.

Purpose

The Internet is a network, or web, of individual computer sites connected by the telephone system. Users are able to move from one site to the next. The sites themselves can be connected. Individual sites have their own purpose: to sell products, to exchange ideas, or to entertain the visitors. Each site has its own purpose, but the Internet as a whole has an overriding purpose that all the users share: the exchange of information. Thus, we find the first general characteristic of a complex system: a unifying *purpose,* but each individual element may have its own purpose as well.

Decentralization and Feedback

The individual Internet sites are usually connected to other sites with which they have some affiliation. The connection may not be direct. Some business-related sites, for instance, have connections for "fun stuff"—favorite sites that have no relationship to the main purpose of the original site. The Internet is *decentralized,* but its elements form a *loosely connected web.* Each site is connected to many other sites, but not to all of the operative sites. There is no central location where one can see the entire structure of the Internet. This is the second general characteristic of a complex system; the Internet is a decentralized structure. There is no single crucial element on which the entire system depends (except for the telephone system, which serves the same purpose as the global ecosystem does for living organisms).

To many observers, decentralization seems inefficient, yet the growth of the Internet has been more rapid than anyone could have planned. It has been estimated that the number of users doubles every 100 days! As sites became more complicated, the technology available became more and more inadequate. One of the original uses of the Internet was to send information. As time went on, users became frustrated with the wait time associated with the original modems. So, modems were developed that enabled users to send data faster. Sites then began to offer more graphical material and larger data files to take advantage of the faster modems. As the data needs grew, modems became inadequate again. Faster modems were developed, along with chips in the individual sites that could handle graphical material more efficiently. In typical capitalist fashion, innovations were developed, which led to more advanced products, which in turn required even more innovation. This leads to the third characteristic of complex systems: *feedback*. The elements of the system influence each other. The influence is decentralized. An innovation will originate in one part of the Internet and spread out from there. No single innovation can influence all of the sites and users of the Internet simultaneously. Many users have the latest, fastest modems, but a host of others are a couple of generations behind.

Adaptation

The feedback itself generates the fourth characteristic: *adaptation*. As its environment changes and the needs of the users change, the system, through its feedback mechanism, creates innovations to adapt to the new demands. It will not produce just one innovation. It will produce many. However, only a few will survive. The innovations that survive are not necessarily the best options, as we will see, but they will be nearly optimal. That is all a system needs. The actual survivors may not be the "fittest," but they are the lucky outcomes of many near-optimal solutions. Though, as Louis Pasteur said, "Chance favors the prepared mind."

Consider the prevalence of Microsoft's MS-DOS system. The dominance of the system can be traced to its acceptance by IBM for its original PC. Many alternative operating systems were in existence at that time; some were more efficient than Microsoft's. However, the selection by IBM, coupled with IBM's open design system for PCs, which was easily cloned, allowed MS-DOS to dominate the software world. The economic environment chose not the best or fittest design, but the near-optimal one. Dominance came for other reasons, including lucky breaks.

Chance

I do not mean to imply that Microsoft's achievements are just lucky. Much hard work and brilliant foresight were involved, but, as in most success stories, Microsoft has had its share of luck. This leads to a fifth characteristic: *chance*—or what we earlier called "surprise." Complex systems can turn chance occurrences into opportunities. On the Internet, connections often occur purely by chance. Yet, the outcome of those connections can be quite far-reaching. Chance allows a decentralized system to generate many solutions. The best of these solutions will be nearly optimal, and one will eventually be chosen.

Rules

Finally, complex systems have *rules* to keep the systems from becoming chaotic. An alternative term is *limitations*. The system cannot do just anything it wants. It must conform to certain limitations that inhibit it for the near term. The Internet has been contained by the technology involved. There is only so much that can be done. As the technology behind the Internet expands, the applications grow but at a controlled pace.

In summary, the following characteristics define a complex system:

1. The system itself has an overriding *purpose*—usually, its own survival.

2. It is a loosely connected, *decentralized* web, but most of its elements have an indirect connection. Knowledge is spread through the elements. No single element knows the big picture.

3. Although it is decentralized, the system has *feedback*. It learns from the experience of its separate elements.

4. The feedback leads to *adaptations* to changes in the system's environment.

5. These adaptations are also decentralized. In order to try out as many innovations as possible, complex systems depend on *chance*. Randomness plays a key role in the ability of a complex system to find a near-optimal innovation. Chance keeps the system from becoming too rigid, and allows it to search for many possible solutions.

6. The system has limitations or *rules* governing its behavior. These rules are themselves adaptable, but they keep the system from becoming chaotic and uncontrollable in its search for adaptive solutions.

The resilience of a complex system depends heavily on its decentralized nature and the role of chance. The combination of these two elements creates the local uncertainties that can cause anxiety when we are dealing with a social system. These uncertainties are more than words, gut feelings, or intuition, but the mathematics behind them is beyond the scope of this book. Interested readers should consult the references for more technical information.

MECHANICS OF COMPLEXITY

How does a loosely connected web generate spontaneous order? A key factor is the number of connections. We often assume that networks are two-dimensional—that is, we assume that a number of elements are laid out in a matrix. Some of these elements are connected to some of their neighbors, but the number of connections is limited. How can such a system generate spontaneous order?

Complex systems have three-dimensional connections. Stuart Kauffman, in *The Origins of Order,* uses an analogy of buttons and threads. Suppose you have 400 buttons, and you begin connecting them one to another with threads. The buttons do not have to be next to each other to be connected. They can be anywhere in the pile, and one button can be connected to many other buttons. Now, suppose we count the size of the largest cluster of buttons. As the ratio of buttons to threads rises, the size of the largest cluster slowly rises. Just before the ratio of threads to buttons crosses 0.50, the size of the largest cluster is about 50 out of the 400 buttons. However, when the ratio of threads to buttons crosses 0.50, something unexpected happens. The size of the largest cluster jumps to about 320 buttons! In physics, this is called a "phase transition." It's the equivalent of when water turns to ice. Suddenly, there is a substantial change. This is a nonlinear reaction. The increase of the largest cluster size indicates that the complexity of the connections has suddenly increased dramatically. If we are dealing with active agents (rather than lifeless buttons), the interactions of the agents also increase dramatically. Suddenly, one agent is connected with about 80 percent of the possible elements rather than 12 percent. The impact from one agent increases accordingly within this universe. The ability of the process to coordinate itself also increases. The transition from a simple system to a complex one happens suddenly, not gradually. Once the transition has occurred, establishing more connections will not necessarily increase the complexity of the process.

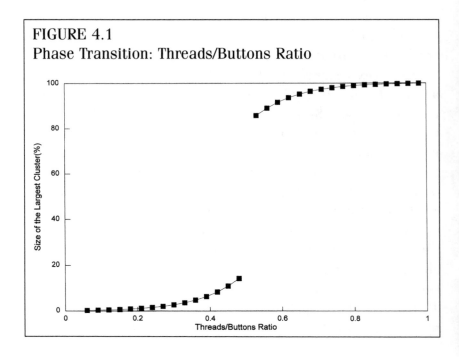

FIGURE 4.1
Phase Transition: Threads/Buttons Ratio

The threads-to-buttons ratio explains how a simple system can suddenly become a richer one, but how does it become "complex"? What else is needed to create "order for free"?

Processes can range from simple to complex. The characterization of these processes can largely be determined by their ability to adapt, or evolve. Ironically, not all "simple" processes are easy to understand. It is also possible to be complicated without being complex.

A Rube Goldberg device is complicated, but not complex.

The Museum of Science (as well as Logan Airport) in Boston has large kinetic sculptures that resemble Rube Goldberg creations. In these sculptures, wooden balls move down ramps, fly through the air, play drums and chimes, and do various other activities. Children and most adults are fascinated by these sculptures, particularly when they try to figure out how everything fits together. Each sculpture is clearly "complicated," but it is not *complex;* in fact, like all mechanical devices, it is extremely structured despite its dynamic nature. Each element must do its part, or the whole structure stops. If conveyor belt A does not pull the balls to the top of the ramp, the structure no longer works. The artist, as central planner, knows what is happening. The rest of the structure merely follows orders. Interestingly, a kinetic sculpture exemplifies what many individuals like to see in organizations or social systems. It has a definite purpose. Each element pulls together so that the structure can achieve this purpose. Finally, it is highly predictable. Nothing is left to chance. There is no uncertainty in a well-oiled machine.

At the other extreme are chaotic processes in which small fluctuations can result in unpredictable results. Ironically, a chaotic process can look a lot simpler than a kinetic sculpture. During his lectures, Dr. Doyne Farmer of the Santa Fe Institute likes to illustrate chaos by releasing an air-filled balloon into the audience. The balloon is propelled as it expels air, and it flies erratically around the room. No matter what we do, this well-defined process cannot be predicted. A small change in air pressure, or the underlying air currents from a heating ventilator, can drastically change the flight path of the balloon. Despite the simplicity of the process, it is completely unpredictable.

How can we have, first, a complicated process that is highly predictable, and then a simple process that is unpredictable? What are the differences?

In the kinetic sculpture, small fluctuations are quickly absorbed. Each time around, a wooden ball may have a slightly different speed than the last time, or its angle when hitting the drum may be different, but those small fluctuations do not mean much. The system is so structured that small variations in the running process are quickly damped out. The process is stable and keeps to its purpose.

The balloon, on the other hand, amplifies any small fluctuations in its environment. It adapts to small changes in the temperature, for instance, by drastically changing its course. However, the instability of the balloon shows that it has no purpose. It merely reacts to changes in its environment in a wildly unpredictable manner.

An adaptive process cannot be at either of these extremes. The structured process has no room for chance. The system is stable as long as fluctuations stay small, but it collapses under large changes. Chaotic systems adapt to changes but are unstable. The complex systems we see around us are between these two extremes. Complex systems are stable *and* adaptive to chance events, even large ones. The Santa Fe Institute has characterized these processes as hovering at *the edge of chaos,* where chance and necessity coexist. The edge of chaos allows a decentralized process where enough connections exist (i.e., the ratio of threads to buttons); a random problem or event will then lead to a search for many possible solutions. Through selection, it chooses a near-optimal solution.

Uncertainty and Freedom

Living as elements within a complex process forces us to deal with the uncertainty inherent in the process. All around us, the search for solutions to problems we are not even aware of goes on. We sense the order behind these seemingly independent and random events, but cannot articulate it. This sense of order causes us anxiety because there is no central planner. Living in a free society such as a democracy or a free-market economy means living with this uncertainty. Reducing uncertainty would mean lowering the number of choices that the system can implement in its search for solutions posed by an ever changing environment. Reductions in the number of options would mean a reduction in adaptability, the very hallmark of a free society.

We can see now why it is so difficult for socialist societies to adapt to free markets, or for countries that once had totalitarian rule (whether communist or fascist) to adopt democracy. Low levels of freedom also mean low levels of uncertainty. The number of options available to citizens in non-free societies is limited, but there is also comfort in the reduction of anxiety. Freedom brings not only responsibility, but uncertainty as to the future. Unprepared for the anxiety that accompanies freedom, many societies slide back into the comfort of less uncertainty and less freedom. Only when they understand that the price of freedom is uncertainty will democracy and free markets take hold.

PART TWO

Free Markets and the
Need for Uncertainty

The solution of the economic problem of society is . . .
always a voyage of exploration into the unknown. . . .
—F.A. Hayek

CHAPTER 5

Subjectivism: "The Economics of Time and Ignorance"

. . . it is always advisable to perceive clearly our ignorance.
—Charles Darwin

The social object of skilled investment should be to defeat the dark forces of time and ignorance which envelope our future.
—John Maynard Keynes

THERE are few fields where uncertainty is more widely discussed and misunderstood than in economics. An entire mathematical discipline, econometrics, has been developed to model uncertainty, and an entire subfield, portfolio theory, was developed to diversify uncertain events. Uncertainty is a regular topic in business circles. Decision making under conditions of uncertainty is the subject of countless articles in academic journals. There is little agreement on the meaning of uncertainty. However, the study of "economic uncertainty" can be divided into two schools: (1) the mainstream (Keynesian) school and (2) the subjectivist, or Austrian school.

61

The Keynesian school dominates economic study in academic circles. Richard Nixon, during his administration, said, "We are all Keynesians, now." There are economic schools besides the Keynesians and the Austrians, but most of the disparate schools define uncertainty in the Keynesian manner. Because uncertainty is our topic, we will lump these groups together as the *mainstream* school, as distinguished from the *Austrian* school.

In general, the mainstream school defines uncertainty in the same manner as probabilists; that is, uncertainty can be measured by assessing the probabilities, the associated risks, and the benefits (or "utility") of all the possible outcomes. We make decisions based on the trade-off of the risks and returns associated with these probabilities. What if the probabilities are unknown? We use subjective probabilities like good Bayesians. Any other approach is *irrational*. Time is irrelevant.

Unfortunately, the real world is quite different from the toy world of economic academia. Only an irrational person would use probabilities based on incomplete information. As we have seen in Part I, the vast majority of our decisions are made in the dark. We do not know the current conditions or all of the possible outcomes of our actions, let alone a set of probabilities. We use heuristics or rules-of-thumb instead. Remember Dilemma 3 in Chapter 2? The "probability" of the Fed's raising interest rates was actually a measure of the similarity of current conditions to past environments. Such decision making is based on rules-of-thumb rather than true probabilities. Because mainstream economics considers these decision-making methods irrational, economic study has been of little use in helping us make better decisions or explaining why we make the decisions we do.

Luckily, a separate school, the Austrian school, is based on a different premise: subjectivism. Subjectivism is not new. In fact, the Austrian school predates the Keynesian school by about 50 years. In the 1930s, the Austrian school competed with the Keynesian school for dominance, but Keynesianism, which promised understanding *and* prediction, won. By correctly formulating a problem, the Keynesians said, we could understand and predict the consequences of our actions. Uncertainty would be reduced to "exogenous" shocks to the economy. The promise to eliminate uncertainty and the ability to find the "right" answers swept aside competing schools of thought. But Keynesianism failed. Economic forecasting has become a joke. Yet, the mainstream school continues to dominate. The hope of prediction has, so far, outweighed the disappointment of experience. The search for the Holy Grail of forecasting continues. Ironically, Keynes himself understood that not all risks could be assessed by probability. He said: "[for] uncertain matters . . . there is no scientific basis on which to form any calculable probability whatever. We simply do not know!" Mirroring the believers of Darwin and evolution, Keynes's followers ignored their founder's insight into the limitations of his own theory and followed the easier route. They embraced probability as a measure of risk in order to make the problems solvable for one right answer.

The Austrian school offers understanding but explicitly says that prediction is at best chancy, and at worst impossible. Uncertainty cannot be eliminated; it is part of the nature of free markets. Mathematical modeling of economic phenomena is a pipe dream. Free markets are too complex for models and predictions. The duty of economics is not to set policy but to understand how free agents, pursuing their own interests, can spontaneously organize into a coherent economic entity. Austrian economics cannot offer the comfort of control that the Keynesian school can. Despite the Keynesian ascendancy, the Austrian school has continued to evolve, and mathematics has finally caught up with its intuitive models. The mathematics of complex systems largely describes the same phenomena as those close to the heart of the Austrian school. If the Austrian description is correct, then economic uncertainty is not only a fact of life in free markets, *it is necessary if markets are to exist at all.* To evolve and adapt, free markets need uncertainty.

WHAT IS SUBJECTIVISM?

The Austrian, or subjectivist, school of economics has been aptly described by the title Gerald P. O'Driscoll and Mario J. Rizzo gave their book: *The Economics of Time and Ignorance.* Ironically, they took their title from Keynes. At its core, the Austrian school believes that economic activity is largely a matter of individual choice and subjective interpretation of events and conditions. The economy (and society in general) is made up of many individuals with separate needs. For the most part, these economic agents act independently and in their own self-interest. However, while their individual interests are ongoing, these agents are operating within a network of other agents who are pursuing related, if not identical, goals. From this loose coupling, organization spontaneously erupts, and innovation emerges.

Suppose that there is a teenager named Jack in your neighborhood. Jack has decided that he needs to make some money to buy a super-light trail bike with an automatic transmission (cost: $500). His parents have refused to buy it for him. Jack decides that there is money to be made in your neighborhood by cutting lawns. He talks to his parents. They agree that he can buy the bike with his own money, and they allow him to use their lawn mower, but he has to buy the gas for the mower. Jack agrees to these conditions. Gas, he finds, will cost him about $1 per lawn. Each lawn will take about an hour and a half to cut. He finds that professional lawn services charge $20 per lawn.

He knows he can beat that, so he decides to charge $15 per lawn. He canvasses the neighborhood and finds five homeowners (including you) who would like to use his services. His earnings per week will come out to $70 (after he pays for gas). The business outlook for the summer is good. Jack makes his money and buys his bike.

This sequence seems perfectly simple and ordinary, but look at what is going on. Jack has a need. He wants to buy a bike, but he does not have the money. He finds a need within the neighborhood—lawn cutting—which is completely independent of his own need. The price of gasoline is set independently of Jack's need, as is the price charged by his competition (the professional lawn services). Jack has no idea how they came up with the $20 price, but he uses this information to set his $15 price. The price is adequate for Jack to realize, as profit, the amount he needs to buy the bike, the price of which has been set without Jack in mind. Yet, despite all of the independent decisions and events going on here, everyone is happy, except perhaps the lawn service company. The neighborhood gets its lawns cut at a reduced price. Gasoline is bought and used. A $500 bicycle is also sold; its manufacture and sale have touched many other industries and lives. Even Jack's parents benefit. Their son earned a new bike without needing their financial help, and he managed to learn a valuable entrepreneurial lesson in the bargain.

How did all of these independent agents know how to interact? Who planned all of this? The answer, of course, is: no one. There was no need for any individual to have all of the information necessary for this system to work. Each of the parties involved—Jack, his parents, the neighbors, the gas company, the lawn service, and the bicycle shop—contributed bits of the total story. The group knows more about the needs of the whole than any one individual.

This simple example can be extrapolated to the entire economy. The exciting and disturbing thing about a free market is that no one knows where it is going or why. Yet, as a whole, the economy continues developing.

This is the crux of the Austrian school's thesis. A free-market economy is made up of independent agents acting in their own self-interest. Each agent is making decisions and acting in real time (as defined in Part I) under conditions of true uncertainty. As they pursue their goals, individuals will need the services of others who have expertise, knowledge, or materials that they do not possess. The individuals interact with other individuals who are also pursuing their own self-interest. However, when the agents interact, the resulting process is more than the sum of the parts. Each agent must compromise some part of his or her activities in order to gain the cooperation of others. No one stands alone. The cooperative nature of the process results in spontaneous organization. The overall structure occurs without planning. No one is deciding who should do what. It all just happens. There is an unspoken agreement that there should be cooperation, and rules are generated to govern the behavior of the participants so that they can trust one another. After a period of time, these rules are formalized and become laws.

The resulting structure has no central planning. There is no authority to dictate the goals each participant should have. This situation has numerous implications. First, that individuals are making decisions based on their own subjective view of current conditions. Thus, their decisions are not rigidly determined by external events or authorities. Because decisions can be based on information that is important only to the individual, it is impossible to predict with complete accuracy what any individual will do in a particular set of circumstances. In fact, under the same basic circumstances, individuals can make different decisions because their subjective views are slightly different.

Suppose, for instance, that you are on a diet. You are traveling on a plane, and the airline has fortunately upgraded you to first class. You missed lunch, and dinner is being served. The dessert today is a special brand of chocolate ice cream. You know that you should not eat it, but it looks very good. Objectively, you admit that you should not take the ice cream. It is against the compact you made with yourself to keep to the diet. The dessert is not good for you. However, you did miss a meal today, so your caloric intake was less than it would have been. The actual outcome of your eating the ice cream is unknown. Will you gain back weight if you eat it, or will this one serving of ice cream be easily absorbed with no weight gain? Will this cheating remain an isolated incident, or are you starting down the path to continued weight gain? In the split second when you make this kind of decision, you can go either way. Your path is not rigorously determined. You can estimate the odds of each possible decision based on your character and how much willpower you have shown in the past. However, a single decision is largely unpredictable. The next day, faced with identical conditions, you might make a different decision. The same sequence occurs if you are making an important decision, such as how to time trades when you are buying stocks, or deciding between mundane choices, such as what kind of sandwich to order for lunch.

The fact that our decisions cannot be predicted because of our feelings at the moment of decision has broad implications. A common guessing game on Wall Street involves trying to predict the Federal Reserve's policy on interest rates. When it must make such a decision, the Fed usually has a long list of conflicting information. Typically, the Fed looks for exceptionally strong economic growth and low unemployment as a basis for saying that current conditions are encouraging inflation pressures to build. The Fed's stated objective is to maintain stable economic growth through price stability. However, economic data are imprecise and often in conflict. Economic data are, in fact, ambiguous, as defined in Chapter 3. How the Fed interprets the data, and makes a final decision, could depend on its mindset *du jour* or how much faith its individual members have in certain items of information. We might be able to say that, given this set of information in the past, the Fed has generally decided to raise (or lower) interest rates. However, that does not reliably predict any actual action at this or any other meeting. The Fed's decision-making process, in the end, is subjective and indeterminate. Even if we know the information that will be examined, we cannot say with certainty that the Fed will take one action or another.

In a free-market economy, individual investors use the same processes. Yet, despite the fact that investors are pursuing their own self-interest, the free market does, in fact, have a structure. It was set up by the participants as a group, though no one individual can take credit or blame for it. No one, including the Fed, the President, the Congress, or the captains of industry can know exactly what is going on in the economy. Moriarty does not exist. Yet, we can feel the *structure,* and we know that the whole continues. We are a part of that whole.

COMPLEXITY AND PURPOSE

In Chapter 4, we discussed complex processes. One of the criteria for a complex process is that it has a *purpose,* or a reason for being. A free market exists so that its members can exchange goods and services with one another. The purpose is to freely move capital from one source to another. The free market must also survive; if a portion of it breaks down, then the system must self-correct. Unlike a structured system—for example, a socialist or a totalitarian state—a free market will self-correct and adapt even if the participants are completely unaware of what is happening. How this happens is discussed more fully below. For now, we can say that a free market fulfills the first criterion for a complex process: It has a goal and it works for its own survival.

IS IT EFFICIENT?

The free world's biggest fear during the Cold War was that communism was more efficient than capitalism. Because of its centralized planning process, a communist state could produce more, at lower cost, than a decentralized capitalist system could produce. Particularly during wartime, this was a concern. The capitalist West detested communism because it trampled on individual rights and subjugated the needs of the individual to the needs of the state. This was a moral and philosophical issue. However, when *efficiency* was the issue, there was little doubt that centralized planning would win out. The industrial revolution and the immense gains it achieved in production occurred because of organization. Efficiency was equated with organization, and there was no doubt that the Soviet Union was highly organized.

Yet, at the end of the Cold War, the opposite was found to be true. The Soviet system became synonymous with *inefficiency*. From Chernobyl to the Mir space station, the West saw examples of the Soviets' inability to innovate and adapt, even when life itself was at stake.

F.A. Hayek, the celebrated Austrian economist and Nobel prize winner, wrote extensively throughout his career that the communist system was doomed to failure, and that free markets would prevail despite a perception that capitalism was unorganized and inefficient. His insights proved prophetic. Communism collapsed for virtually all of the reasons he had cited as far back as 60 years ago. Hayek believed that in a system as complex as an economy, a decentralized structure would prove to be more adaptive, more innovative, and, eventually, more efficient than one that has a central planner. Why? A free-market economy gives order for free. The language and mathematics of complexity were not available to him, but Hayek stated that a complex system such as a free market would spontaneously organize and generate innovation within itself, without a central planner. The reason was tied to the conditions under which we, the participants in the economy, make decisions. We must make decisions in real time under conditions of true uncertainty. Without those conditions, our adaptive way of life could not exist.

CHANGE

We now approach the hallmark of the Austrian school of economics and a further link to complexity theory. In a free market, not only is order spontaneously generated, but change comes from within. In the jargon of economists, change is endogenous. The need for change is caused by the inability of the participants to fully coordinate their activities. As we said earlier, individuals working in a free market are loosely coupled to others as they pursue their separate agendas. Their own actions, though, are determined by their subjective interpretations of conditions and events. This diversity of opinion makes it impossible for the agents to interact with perfect efficiency. Usually, the coordination is reasonable. Eventually, needs become divergent and serious gaps appear in the coordination effort. Sometimes, the gaps are small; at other times, they precipitate a "crisis." When a crisis happens, entrepreneurs step in and generate the change that is needed. Thus, change comes from within the system and serves the needs of its economic agents. This is different from "change for change's sake," where powerful individuals try to impose unneeded change. For instance, there is a general feeling that Madison Avenue determines fashion in the United States. There is little evidence to support this claim. True fashion reflects tastes rather than shapes them. For instance, in the late 1960s, there was an attempt to make skirts longer after women had worn them extremely short. Despite extensive advertising, women did not consider long skirts attractive, and rejected them for another couple of years. Lasting change is quite different from a short-term fad.

A recent example of entrepreneurial spirit is tied to the growth of the World Wide Web. The Web is based on the concept of hypertext links: a word in one document allows you to "jump" from that document to another. As originally conceived, hypertext links work like the Help facility in most software. You may be reading a document about the composition of the universe and find a reference to dark matter. Dark matter may be a keyword; by clicking on it, you may jump to a different document that describes dark matter in detail. Hypertext also allows you to jump from one Web site to another.

The development of the Web started at CERN in Geneva, Switzerland. Tim Berners-Lee and his followers created the Hypertext Transfer Protocol (HTTP), which standardized the ability for sites to reference one another. In the early pre-graphic days, hypertext was considered the wave of the future, but it was difficult to use and code. A Web browser called Mosaic was developed in 1993 by Marc Andreessen at the National Center for Supercomputing Applications at the University of

Illinois. The familiar ability to jump through point-and-click graphics originated with Mosaic. Andreessen and others founded Netscape in 1994, and Mosaic became the Navigator. The ability to jump through the graphic interface made the use of the Web much easier. This was followed by automated Hypertext Markup Language (HTML) programs. The Web now dominates the Internet. To some people, it *is* the Internet.

There can be little doubt that the Web browser has profoundly impacted the way the world communicates information. Thus, change is adaptation of a system or process to a changing environment.

The need for change arises because inefficiencies in the process (that is, inefficient coordination) present opportunity for profit. Entrepreneurs, seeing these opportunities within the competitive environment, move to take advantage of them. Thus, the decentralized structure of a free-market environment generates change because competition rewards those who can adapt and innovate. Entrepreneurs are then encouraged to search for solutions to problems.

CREATIVE DESTRUCTION

In a free market, the search for inefficiencies is continuous and ongoing. Cycles can be identified. In the 1930s and 1940s, economist Joseph Schumpeter suggested that cycles develop through the concept of "creative destruction."

In Schumpeter's view, declines in economic activity occur when coordination within the economy reaches a crisis—when large corporations can no longer adapt to changes in the economic environment, or when excess in the cycle reaches a turning point. The financial crisis that began to grip Southeast Asia in 1997 is a recent example of a cycle reaching a breaking point. The so-called Asian "Tigers"—South Korea, Thailand, and Indonesia—had been the fastest growing economies in the world. Global financial institutions, perceiving the Tigers as sources of growth, eagerly began to lend them more money, which led to further growth. Investments were based on contacts with powerful families or individuals, rather than financial projections. For instance, Peregrine Securities, in Hong Kong, lent a large sum to an Indonesian taxi company because it was owned by the sister of Indonesian President Suharto. The loan was unsecured. When the Indonesian currency collapsed, the taxi company was unable to repay its loan. Peregrine went bankrupt.

The entire region, built on large amounts of credit, could no longer support local currencies. Most Asian currencies dropped in value relative to the U.S. dollar. Because the loans were payable in U.S. dollars, most institutions could not repay them. The entire region, built on many bad loans, began sliding into a severe economic decline. Its extent and length are still unknown. Many of the weaker institutions will fail. Those that are more stable will hit hard times but will survive.

The United States faced a similar crisis during the Great Depression of the 1930s. The results were: tighter banking regulations and stricter rules for investment and speculation in the capital markets. The Great Depression saw the birth of many industries and the death of others, but a more stable environment emerged from the chaos. There is no reason to doubt that Southeast Asia will see a similar transformation if the painful but necessary reforms are implemented.

The excesses in Southeast Asia's system brought about a crisis that now sets the stage for innovation and change. The Soviet system, by contrast, could not adapt. It died and must be replaced by a different system.

FREE MARKETS AND COMPLEXITY

The Austrian school of economics has roots going back over 100 years. Complexity theory, dealing with the physical sciences, has arisen in the past 20 years. Both concepts were developed independently, but they share many relationships. The important characteristics of complex systems, described in Chapter 4, also show up in the Austrian view of economic process.

The first and most important link is the *decentralized* nature of the process. As in any complex system, economic agents have a loose relationship to one another. They have both individual and common goals. However, no "top down" bureaucratic organization is involved. Instead, knowledge and activity are spread among the participants. In a physical system, such as an organism, each part fulfills its own particular function while supplying something necessary to the whole. This generates the second relationship, *feedback*. The activity of each economic participant affects the others.

However, the coordination among the participants is incomplete because each interprets information in a different way, which leads to the development of inefficiencies in the economic process. These inefficiencies create innovation as entrepreneurs take advantage of the changed conditions. Innovation causes the system to *adapt* to the new environment, affirming yet another tie to complexity theory.

Much of the innovation depends on luck, or *chance*—another important element of complex systems. Innovators sometimes stumble into opportunities. Often, what separates a successful entrepreneur from a big talker is recognition of an opportunity, plus the persistence to follow it through.

Finally, an economic system has *rules*. In a natural system, these rules take the form of natural law, but even a free market has rules to ensure that the competitive nature of the free market remains intact. Unfortunately, an unregulated market usually ends up as a monopoly, the antithesis of a free market.

Each of these characteristics was discussed in Chapter 4. In this chapter, we briefly noted their relevance to the Austrian view of free markets. In the following chapters, we will look at these relationships in more depth. However, an overriding characteristic deals with competition. As we saw in Chapter 2, competition needs a high level of uncertainty in order for the process to remain competitive. A process with low uncertainty becomes predictable. In free markets, this result is even more prevalent. A "sure thing" is either rigged or regulated, but it has no place in a competitive environment.

CHAPTER 6

Diversity and Knowledge

. . . specks of knowledge are scattered through a vast emptiness of ignorance, and everything depends upon how solid the individual specks are, and on how powerfully linked and coordinated they are with one another.

—Thomas Sowell

I don't want knowledge. I want certainty!

—David Bowie

IN Chapter 3, we asked whether knowledge is knowable, and we discussed the differences among types of knowledge. In this chapter, we will examine how society retains and distributes knowledge. We tend to think of our knowledge as a repository, like a library. All of the information is there; it just needs to be looked up. We also tend to think that "those in charge" have access to all of the information necessary for "the big picture." However, in a large complex process such as a free-market economy, no one person is in charge. The Austrian school of economics contends that the free market divides knowledge among the individual participants so that the whole knows more than the parts. Each participant values information differently because each has different goals and objectives. Each participant then keeps only that part of the puzzle that is relevant to his or her interests. However, in the aggregate, the participants in the economy know more than any individual can or will know. This diversification by *decentralization* of the social stock of knowledge allows a free market to adapt and evolve more efficiently than a directed economy.

In contrast, the mainstream school assumes that everyone has the same information and values it in the same way. In essence, mainstream economics says that all the economic players are *homogeneous;* the Austrians say that individuals are *heterogeneous.* This difference has far-reaching consequences. Homogeneity makes analysis easier, but heterogeneity allows for complexity. Thus, each model creates a different type of uncertainty. As we shall see, the mainstream school's assumption of homogeneity implies that market prices change randomly. Uncertainty is limited to the probability of a negative surprise and is again a statistician's ideal. However, when investors are heterogeneous, *true* uncertainty not only exists but is necessary for the system to function. Without true uncertainty, there can be no competition and no free market.

MARKET EFFICIENCY

Western science is based on study and understanding through reductionism; that is, the best way to understand a large and complex process is to break it down into smaller and smaller pieces. The problem is then easier to handle, and the process as a whole will be the sum of the pieces. Nuclear physics, particularly particle physics, is the ultimate expression of this ideal. Particle physics—the study of the composition of matter at the smallest subatomic level—is viewed as a potential source of knowledge that will help us understand the structure of the universe. (Talk about studying the very small to understand the very large!) In economics, this tradition has been maintained through the construct of an archetypal "rational" person who represents an average of all the participants, a model of the group's behavior. Individuality is subsumed by the average consumer. When free markets are defined by recognizing the contributions of the individual (particularly the entrepreneur), why are people made into faceless averages? Answer: It makes the math easier. With the rational person concept, economists can represent the entire economy through single numbers called aggregates. The behavior of millions can be entered into forecasting equations as one variable. The problem of economic analysis becomes radically simplified, and forecasting becomes possible.

The Efficient Market Hypothesis (EMH) is one of the more conspicuous examples of the reductionist approach. The EMH is a theory (not a "hypothesis" as its name suggests) that attempts to explain why changes in stock prices are unpredictable. First, the theory has its own definition of rationality: Investors wish to maximize their expected return for a given level of risk. That seems reasonable enough. Second, all investors have access to the same information and process it in the same way. Because of these two conditions, market prices are *efficient* (they already reflect all the knowledge that is knowable) and changes in stock prices reflect new information, instantaneously. As a consequence, changes in stock prices are random and cannot be anticipated or profited from.

Market efficiency is a very convenient state. The assumption that markets are efficient allows a battery of statistical tests and forecasting tools that depend on the postulated random nature of stock price movements. The entire field of portfolio theory has been developed around this area of study and has won Nobel prizes. The whole artifice depends on the assumption that investors are rational, on average, and so the market can be treated on the whole as rational and efficient.

A number of beliefs are embedded in this assumption. The first is that different investors value information in the same manner. The second is that investors need the same information and react to it accordingly. It does not matter whether they are security analysts, day traders, portfolio managers, or the Beardstown Ladies. Information is information. It is a commodity. However, a more insidious belief is a consequence of these other beliefs. It involves the economic concept of expectations.

In economics, prices are set based on what people expect will happen in the future. If the individual is indeed the "rational" person postulated by standard theory, these "rational expectations" can follow only one route—the route followed by all rational investors. Thus, the market, in aggregate, acts like a single rational person as defined by economists.

This view has been used for a number of years and has proved useful. Thanks to the concept of economic rationality, models of aggregate economic behavior have been developed. Simple models of markets have also been developed, and they have helped us to understand concepts of risk versus rewards. The famous option pricing formula of Fischer Black and Myron Scholes was based on the fundamental concept of rational investors. However, two important elements are missing from the theory: (1) the goals of individual participants, and (2) the competition they generate, in order to profit in a free market. Without these elements, we no longer have the motivations that define a free market: the need for profit, and the capacity for loss. In making market participants homogeneous and uniform, the market mechanism has been simplified into something completely removed from reality.

Finally, the rational person approach has eliminated uncertainty from the market process. Everyone has the same information, values it in the same way, and has the same goals, so there is no incentive to trade with one another, whether the object of trade is stocks, bonds, pork bellies, or Beanie Babies. We have sacrificed the micro elements in the market and are left holding the macro.

Unfortunately, if markets actually worked this way, the result would not be stability at all. Instead, there would likely be extreme volatility, panics, and crashes on a regular basis.

The stock market, for instance, is one of the largest and most liquid of markets. Investors regularly buy and sell shares in corporations. These shares are, in fact, pieces of a company. They entitle the holder to some portion of the profits that are paid out as dividends. If a company increases its profits, a share in that company is worth more, and demand will make the price rise. However, in the stock market, investors also have access to information as to companies' future earnings. That is, there will be general knowledge about a new product coming to market, or the salability of existing products. Taking into account these various factors, investors will decide what price is "fair," given the earnings prospects of the company.

However, receiving payments out of future earnings is not the only reason people buy and sell shares. Some "investors" buy and sell shares because they expect others to do the same in the near future. These individuals, believing that they have more information than the market as a whole, will buy a stock before the prices rise, or will sell a stock before prices fall. Because their speculation in the stock market is based on what they think other people wish to do, they are working from a slightly different set of information than those who buy or sell based on a firm's long-term earnings prospects. John Maynard Keynes, the father of the mainstream school of economics, was, ironically, a successful speculator. He equated the stock market with a beauty contest that was run in the newspapers of his day.

The beauty contest worked like this. Each day, the newspaper ran the pictures of a number of contestants. Those who picked the contestant that received the most votes from a panel of judges won a prize. In this case, Keynes said, the participants are not necessarily choosing the individual that they personally think is the most beautiful; instead, they are choosing the one that they think everyone else will pick to be the most beautiful. This is, of course, an earlier version of Thaler's number game, discussed in Chapter 2. Speculators resemble judges who are trying to pick the winner in a beauty contest. They are trying to anticipate others' choices rather than choosing based on the "fundamentals."

In the stock market, speculators choose various methods for trying to anticipate what everyone else is trying to do. Those methods, generally referred to as "technical analysis," amount to looking at numerous charts and tables to decide whether the trend is in one direction or another.

Imagine what the markets would be like if they actually were dominated by short-term investors who use technical analysis. When the market started to go up, they would, of course, buy. Because of the open access to the same information, everyone else would also start buying, and the price would continue rising until the buyers had depleted their funds. Without buyers, the price of the stock would start falling, which would be taken as a signal to sell. The selling would continue until all shares were sold. We can see that this process is not working. There must be a minimum level at which investors stop selling. This level is generally set by the fundamentals. If everyone knew what the minimum value of a stock should be, the selling would stop when the price reached that level, and the buying would start. The price would fluctuate wildly between its upper and lower bounds.

This does happen on occasion (we will discuss why in a moment), but it is not the general state of affairs, even in the newest emerging markets. What is wrong with this view of the markets?

DIVERSITY OF KNOWLEDGE

The mainstream model is based on homogeneous expectations and valuation. It does not take into account the actual mechanics of the trading through which investments are made. All of the investors know what information is available, how everyone interprets it, and what they will do with the knowledge. Despite the certainty under which everyone is operating, we have extreme volatility. Suppose we take a different approach. As in Ekeland's simple poker game in Chapter 2, we will find that stabilizing the market process requires the introduction of an element of uncertainty.

Suppose we substitute for the homogeneous investor of the mainstream model. Instead, we say that each investor has his or her own needs for investment. Some investors wish to profit from the short-term fluctuations that result from crowd behavior. Others wish to save for their children's college fund. Still others are institutional investors who are responsible for a pension trust that will pay out a stream of benefits to current retirees while accumulating funds for the baby boomers who will retire in the future.

Note that each investor has a personal "investment horizon," defined as the time selected to profit from the investment. A speculator has a short horizon; it can be as long as a day, or as short as a few minutes. The horizon of people saving for college tuition can range from 18 years to 1 year, depending on the current age of their children. A pension fund has a perpetual horizon that can be quantified; generally, the projection is 20 to 30 years into the future. Given the different goals (temporal and specific) for each investor, it is not surprising that each would have a different information set. The speculator continues to trade based on trends. The investors with longer horizons will tend toward more fundamental information; they are concerned with the earnings prospects and potential gain in the value of the company over several business cycles. Hence, a pension fund should use criteria that is different from those of the speculator, though each will trade with the other. What the speculator considers a poor trend could be good news to the pension fund. Suppose a stock price is declining purely for technical reasons. The speculator would consider this a reason to sell. However, over a 20-year period, the current price could be quite attractive, so the pension fund would buy. The speculator sells, while the pension plan buys on the same information. Realistically, this is how the market operates. Because the participants have diverse goals, they value information in diverse and idiosyncratic ways.

As long as these conditions persist, the stock market is stable. Its fluctuations, or runs up and down, continue, but the transition of capital is done in a stable and orderly manner.

Why do wild fluctuations or "crashes" occur, as they did in 1873, 1929, 1962, 1979, 1987, 1989, and 1997? In each case, something happened that made the long-term investors doubt their ability to value securities for the long term. In 1987, for instance, the rise in interest rates caused by the rapid decline of the dollar made the future state of the U.S. economy questionable. Long-term investors either stopped trading or began trading based on short-term information. The market, in effect, became homogeneous in the manner suggested by the mainstream model. The result was extreme volatility.

Diversifying the investment horizons of the market participants generally results in a more stable market environment. *The stability comes from diversifying the knowledge base of the market participants.* Each investor has a personal set of criteria, and no other investors can know the strategy and goals that are involved. Diversifying the knowledge base increases the uncertainty of the market participants and lowers the risk of wild fluctuations. Increased uncertainty lowers risk and increases the stability of the process.

AUSTRIAN ECONOMICS AND KNOWLEDGE

The Austrian school has a similar view of knowledge in economics. There are two important contexts: (1) the importance of learning, and its impact on the economic process, and (2) the division of knowledge among the market participants themselves. We can see here in high relief the difference between the Austrian and mainstream schools. The mainstream school not only considers participants homogeneous in their interpretation and gathering of knowledge, it also ignores the impact of learning on the economic process. Both omissions make the mathematics behind the mainstream school much easier to manipulate. However, they take the models far from reality. In fact, they become like this old joke:

Walking along the street one night, a man comes across a drunk who is on his hands and knees under a streetlight. The drunk announces that he is searching for his lost keys. The man asks where the drunk was when he last remembered holding his keys. The drunk points off into the darkness. The man asks,

"Why are you looking here, then?" The drunk replies, "Because the light is better over here."

The mainstream school continues to look where the light is best, even though the actual answer is elsewhere. The desire for convenience can overshadow the quest for truth, which is why economics continues to be the "dismal" science.

Convenience is not the only problem. There is also a prejudice that learning is a deterministic process—that is, learning can be modeled as a preprogrammed response to specific stimuli. Part of the problem seems to be confusion between "learning" and "schooling." It is true that most of us receive our training in the classroom. Learning in this context is a matter of following a preprogrammed set of criteria. However, if we define learning as discovering solutions to problems, or the limitations we encounter in real life, then the type of learning that is accomplished in school is quite inadequate. This is how we differentiate schooling from learning: In our schooling, we are taught from the existing social stock of knowledge; when learning, we discover new solutions to problems. In fact, Winston Churchill said, "My education has been interrupted only by my schooling." Here again, we find the need for uncertainty in a creative process. In schooling, there is no uncertainty for the student (except, perhaps, in the grades received). The stock of knowledge that is to be communicated is known well in advance. Contrast that with "on the job" learning. The individual must progress within a state of uncertainty toward a solution that may not even exist. As Karl Popper said, "When we speak of a problem we do so almost always from hindsight. A man who works on a problem can seldom say clearly what his problem is (unless he has found a solution). . . . "

Learning indicates an accumulation of knowledge that expands over a long, perhaps lifelong, time frame. Learning is a continuous process done in real time. Thus, future learning is dependent on what has already been learned. This view of learning in real time has broad implications for the concept of innovation, as we shall see in Chapter 8.

In addition to learning, the distribution of knowledge is viewed differently by the Austrian school. The mainstream school assumes that all participants have the same knowledge, interpret it the same way, and have the same goals and investment horizon. In the Austrian view, participants are individuals who have their own goals, their own horizons, and so, their own stock of knowledge. Individuals do not need to have all of the available knowledge; much of it is irrelevant to their goals. Most of us consider our cars simply vehicles for transportation, and we use them as such. The mysteries of fuel injection and the function of fuzzy logic processors within transmissions are irrelevant to our daily lives. So it is with other types of knowledge as well. We take only what we need. Each economic participant has a piece of the social stock of knowledge. No one has the whole universe of what might be learned. Thus, in the Austrian view, it is inefficient to assign a group or a committee or an individual to set policy for the economy as a whole, because no unit possesses as much information as the whole itself. Yet, because of the loose connection that all individuals have with one another through their *overlapping* stock of knowledge, the economy functions as an entity. This gives us the feeling that the economy is being controlled, yet we do not know by whom. The collective members control the process, not one individual.

Here is where the connection between the Austrian school and complexity theory becomes most pronounced. A key requirement for a complex process is a loose connection among the participants. When enough connections are established, the ratio of "threads to buttons" crosses its critical threshold, and most of the participants are indirectly connected with the others. In the economy, we now see that the physical basis for the loose connection is *the stock of knowledge*. It is not common to all individuals, but is instead spread among them. The overlaps in knowledge, and so in goals, become the loose connection necessary for spontaneous organization to occur. Hence, we have the "invisible hand" of Adam Smith as well as the bull and bear markets of Wall Street.

Such a loose connection among the participants also creates a fair amount of uncertainty. No one knows how much the other participants know, nor how other individuals with other goals and knowledge will react to or be affected by our decisions. What we do know is that, directly or indirectly, no one is immune in a free market. Contrary to popular myth or belief, a free market requires a high degree of interconnection, not a rugged individual standing alone in freedom.

COMMUNICATION

The Austrian school is also called the Subjectivist school. The Austrians believe that what differentiates individual elements in the economy is their subjective interpretation of information. This occurs because each individual has personal goals and objectives. Consider the implications for communication. If everyone has access to the same stock of information, necessary or unnecessary, what is known would eventually be communicated. Knowledge would indeed become homogeneous. However, the Austrians contend that because our goals and objectives are different, we subjectively interpret the information we receive. For instance, the Bible is read by all Christians. However, the same words mean different things to different people. Not only are there multiple sects of Christianity, there are also countless individual interpretations of the same text. Most non-Christian religious organizations have the same characteristics of internal diversity. If humans are unable to interpret their own sacred texts in a uniform manner, how can they interpret economic information in unison?

In everyday life, ask three people to describe a particular event, and you will get three different versions. This happens with great regularity even if the event is important. One of the reasons that conspiracy theories continue to cloud the JFK assassination is that the eyewitness accounts are so varied. Many people saw smoke or heard a shot coming from the "grassy knoll." An even larger number heard nothing. Even the number of shots fired is in dispute. Of those interviewed, 65 percent heard three shots; 45 percent, including Jacqueline Kennedy, heard only two. Numerous literary works and films have depicted this side of human nature to great effect. One of Akira Kurosawa's great masterpieces, *Rashomon,* tells the same story three times, from the points of view of three eyewitnesses. In each retelling, the story is completely different. The story is about an investigation of a rape. In one account, the man the woman was with is to blame. A second account says that a stranger victimized both the man and the woman. A third version makes the woman the aggressor because she taunted the man. Each narration reveals the point of view of the narrator, even as each uses the same facts.

Communication also gets back to our discussion in Chapter 3: Information can be ambiguous. Subjectively, we try to relate information or events to things we know or have experienced. In *Rashomon,* the state of events clearly was in the minds of the beholders. Because the real "truth" may never be determined, there are limits on how much of human decision making can be modeled, or how many actions of humans can be predicted. As we saw in Chapter 3, more information may not result in less ambiguity. More information may only raise more questions.

Thus, information, even when it is transmitted to everyone, will be interpreted in many different ways. For this reason, the heterogeneous beliefs of individuals cannot be reduced below a certain level, and uncertainty can never be eliminated in society.

The interpretation of information may also depend on the way in which the information is presented. In the past 30 years, there have been interesting developments in the area of behavioral psychology. Kahneman, Slovic, and Tversky, in a pioneering study, found that the way we interpret information can be biased by the way it is presented. Interpretive presentation, also called *framing*, has been used by salespeople since the dawn of capitalism. For instance, suppose I told you to choose between two bets: (1) a sure loss of $100, or (2) a 5 percent chance of losing $10,000 and a 95 percent chance of losing nothing. Most people would consider both choices poor bets. However, suppose I asked you if you would insure a $10,000 engagement ring for $100. Most people would consider the insurance reasonable and advisable. By framing the bet as "insurance," it now becomes a prudent action.

The Behaviorists have also produced a proof of behavior that the Austrians have endorsed for some time: The order in which people receive information is significant. Kahneman, Slovic, and Tversky found that people estimate that $30 \times 29 \times \ldots \times 1$ will yield a larger number than $1 \times 2 \times 3 \times \ldots \times 30$ simply because of the order in which the numbers are presented.

Other studies have supported the notion that the heterogeneous nature of the information stock of society cannot be reduced beyond a certain level. Because of the nature of communication and the reception of knowledge, there can never be a time when all members of a society interpret the knowledge they have in the same way, even if it were possible for all of them to acquire the same information. As O'Driscoll and Rizzo state, "Even in equilibrium, then, not everyone will know the same things." The equilibrium they are referring to is the equilibrium of the mainstream school.

Thus, an "efficient" market, in the sense of the Efficient Market Hypothesis, is impossible. Any price could never reflect everyone's information even if everyone had the same information.

Why is this insight critical for economics? Because it makes a free market a complex process. If static equilibrium were ever achievable, a free market could not be a complex process. The loose link involves the overlapping of nonidentical information. This, in turn, enables self-organization to occur. Thus, we can see that Austrian economics allows for one of the central tenets of a complex process: a loose coupling between the participants, which allows for a decentralized nature. In the next chapter, we will examine how three other required elements for complexity arise from the main credo of free-market economics: Competition.

CHAPTER 7

Crisis and Competition: Creative Destruction in Free Markets

Chance favors the prepared mind.
                                        —Louis Pasteur

Even if you're on the right track, you'll get run over if you just sit there.
                                        —Will Rogers

SCENARIO: You belong to an organization that changed the way men dress. You created a short-sleeved business suit. It became the rage. Everywhere you looked, men were wearing short-sleeved business suits. The company became prosperous. Stock options made all the owners millionaires. Suddenly, it was over. No one wants short-sleeved business suits now. Your business, built on that one idea, has begun to fall apart. What do you do?

Usually, an organization goes through a number of stages when a crisis hits. The first three stages are: (1) denial

("Everything is under control"); (2) fixing the blame ("We have investigated the problem, and have found those responsible"); and (3) punishing the guilty (various methods: guillotining the royal family, burning the witches, ritual suicides, prison terms, golden handshakes). After these stages peter out, the *real* search for solutions starts—at least, that is what happens to organizations that fail. Those that survive look for solutions that are either apart from or concurrent with stages 1, 2, and 3.

In a free market, the search for solutions always looks disorganized. No one appears to be in charge of a problem situation. There is always pressure to "appoint a committee," which immediately appoints a subcommittee to find a solution. A central authority can often help in the search, but usually the participants slowly find their way after exploring a number of blind alleys. Interestingly, the solution is often forthcoming simultaneously from different sources. The answer is always obvious in retrospect, but, while the search goes on, uncertainty and its accompaniment—anxiety—run at high levels. There is always a feeling that there must be a better way to at least reduce the uncertainty. Unfortunately, that is exactly what should *not* be done. Reducing uncertainty eliminates an important element of the free-market process: competition.

COMPETITION

If only one word could be used to define free markets, it would be *competition*. A similar concept in nature is called *survival*. The flow of capital gives a free market its purpose, and the sharing of knowledge gives the participants their relationship, but competition requires the components that make a free market complex. Competition produces feedback, which leads to innovation and adaptation. However, the process of discovery requires chance as much as genius. In combination, these elements lead to a process that is always in a high state of uncertainty. In fact, sheer survival in a competitive environment requires a high level of uncertainty. There is, after all, no easier prey than one that is predictable. Con men call their victims "marks" because their predictability makes them easily identifiable.

Like all complex elements, competition has consequences as well as benefits. Competition leads to crisis, the dark side of free-market economics. Despite this drawback, competition is the final element that leads to a free market's complexity. Remember, complexity is a *process*. It is always dynamic, always changing and adapting. There is no such thing as static equilibrium. Equilibrium is a *dynamic* process in which the global or typical characteristics are stable, but the details are ever changing. Competition keeps the process moving. The goal of competition might be: the food in an ecosystem, an optimal solution in a neural network, or the available capital in a free market. The competition cannot be unconstrained, however. There are always rules to ensure that cooperation continues. Cooperation is necessary to maintain the loose links we examined in the previous chapter. In this chapter, we will look at the feedback and adaptation that grow out of economic competition, and the pain of economic crisis.

DISCOVERY

Participants in a free market are loosely connected by overlapping knowledge and overlapping goals. In the example of Jack and his lawn-cutting business, the goal of making money to pay for a bicycle was loosely connected with the store's desire to sell the bicycle and with the neighborhood's desire to save money. All three goals were loosely connected, but only Jack was aware of all three components. If we were to list the goals of *everyone* involved, we would have to include those of the bicycle manufacturer, the steel maker, the tire maker—the list goes on and on. No one on the list knows all of the details of this transaction; no one needs to know them. However, the overlapping goals make the system work without a central planner. "Competition," Hayek said, "means decentralized planning by many separate persons."

As we expand this image to include the broader economy, we come to the concept of the *entrepreneur*. In the 1990s, we celebrate the entrepreneur, but the definition used in formal Austrian economics is different from the one referred to by the popular press. To Austrians, an entrepreneur is someone who elicits a *creative* response to a change in the economic environment. According to Joseph Schumpeter, there are two types of response to environmental changes. The first is an *adaptive* response: An economic entity "reacts to a protective duty by its expansion within existing practice." In other words, a corporation modifies the way it currently does business, in response to changes in economic conditions. Most of what passes for "innovation" falls under the adaptive role. The second type of response, a *creative* response, occurs when an entity does something that is "outside the range of existing practice."

In the early days of personal computers, it became clear that the interface between users and PCs was appropriate only for computer geeks. This was true for IBM-compatible and Apple II systems—the two dominant types of PCs at that time. For the PC to become generally accepted by the public, like a radio, it needed to become easier to use. The initial response by users of IBM-compatible machines resulted in improved software, but problems remained with attaching a new printer to a PC, or with finding and installing software that did not conflict with other applications already in use. New games might work perfectly, but games previously installed would stop dead because of "conflicts" in the software. The problem was addressed on the surface: "How do we make software easier to use?" The broader need—to make PCs accessible to nongeeks—was left unanswered. This was a classic adaptive response.

Apple addressed this problem by creating a complete graphical "point and click" interface for the Macintosh computer system. Hardware was made automatically compatible by a process called "plug and play." There were other problems with the original Macintosh, but Apple's response to the problem was innovative and truly creative. All of the current Windows technology is some variant on the original Apple Macintosh design.

Competition drove the changes and the ingenuity that finally made PCs more than toys for geeks. Unfortunately, the original innovator, Apple, fell behind the newcomers' pace. That symptom of free-market ascendancy will be addressed later.

The evolution of PC operating systems illustrates the difference between adaptive and creative response. The introduction and growth of the PC itself is an example of what Schumpeter called "creative destruction": how the economy, through entrepreneurs, resolves a crisis through innovation. The outdated method is not replaced immediately, as is often assumed. Instead, the new and the old grow, side by side. So it was with PCs.

A crisis of centralization led to the development of PCs. Until the 1970s, computer processing required large mainframe computers and an army of programmers. Suppose a company's Public Relations department needed something as simple as mailing labels for all clients located in Ohio. A request was sent to the Data Processing department, which would put the request in a queue, and eventually print the labels. Fulfillment took about a week. The department name, the *Data* Processing department, was endemic. Computing and the handling of data were considered synonymous.

"Time-sharing" companies allowed individuals and corporations to dial into their mainframe computers via remote terminals. The users were not merely firms that could not afford a mainframe; they were also suppliers of specialized services.

In the early 1980s, I worked for a time-sharing company called Interactive Data Corporation (IDC). In those days, the only way to gain access to historical stock prices, balance sheet information, and software was through a time-sharing company like IDC. IDC applications included spreadsheets, accounting systems, modeling, and graphics. The process was complete, fairly easy to use, and *very* expensive. The company made money by offering subscriptions to the databases, but that was a small part of its revenue. Its primary income came from charges for computer time. The more processing you needed, the more money you spent. Such was the world of centralized data processing.

The PC offered *decentralized* data processing. Each user had a computer, so only the data were needed. IDC knew it had a problem. In the beginning, PCs were not powerful enough for most applications. Complex econometric models could not be run on a standard PC. But the technology caught up eventually. IDC could foresee that end users would no longer need IDC's mainframe to process data. They would need only the data. Over a number of years, that prediction came true. In the beginning, PCs were used for simple applications but the mainframe was still needed for the more elaborate problems. Then IDC watched its business fade. It could not come up with a solution that maintained its data-processing capabilities along with its data, so the time-sharing profits died. IDC still lives as a data vendor, but its days as a data-processing company are over.

The time-sharing business was fine when it started. It offered users an opportunity to do things they could not do on their own. However, it became inefficient and bureaucratic. Changes to the software took weeks or months, or were not done at all. That whole mode of doing business was destroyed and replaced with a creative solution. Centralized data processing gave way to decentralization.

Entrepreneurs picked up the slack. Lotus and Microsoft took over the spreadsheet business. PCs devoured centralized word processing, which had replaced the typewriter just a couple of years before. Businesses disappeared and were replaced by more efficient, cheaper alternatives.

This is the way of the free market. This particular sequence created a crisis in an entire industry. The same pattern can be found in the general business cycle.

THE BUSINESS CYCLE

To the Austrians, the business cycle is a matter of coordination. Individuals are trying to mesh their plans in order to meet separate objectives. In particular, producers are attempting to coordinate their production and development activities in order to satisfy the needs of consumers. In a "perfect market," these activities would be exactly met. Strangely, the mainstream school calls this "perfect competition," even though the concept eliminates competition. When producers and consumers exactly mesh their plans, there is no need for competition. Instead of perfect competition, the theory should have been called "perfect coordination." An important assumption is built into the perfect competition model: All parties have the same information and value it in the same way. Only if knowledge is homogeneous will a state of perfect competition exist. However, we saw in the previous chapter that this is impossible in reality. Not only do individuals possess an incomplete set of information, they also do not interpret their common information in the same way. In addition, because consumers and producers are working in real time, as we defined earlier, the choices they make will vary from time to time, even if the conditions are virtually identical. Therefore, no matter what they do, the participants cannot perfectly mesh their objectives and plans.

In real time, with heterogeneous participants, plans can never be perfectly coordinated. Tastes change. Conditions change. Producers can never be entirely sure of what consumers want. Using trial and error, producers try to find a solution. Remember New Coke? Coca-Cola felt that Pepsi was making inroads because consumers wanted a sweeter drink than "classic" Coke. That turned out to be untrue, and New Coke was finally phased out. This trial-and-error process produces a variety of consumer products that compete with one another for shelf space. One product may dominate a market with a majority share, but the heterogeneous nature of consumers' tastes, combined with the searching function of producers, ensures that variety will continue.

The business environment is filled with uncertainty. Producers are trying to anticipate the next "hot" product. Consumers are balancing health and price elements against personal tastes and occasional self-indulgence. Even after a product becomes mature, uncertainty continues in the sales field. There is always a new soft drink to try. Without uncertainty, we would not have variety.

In the aggregate, product cycles lead to business cycles. In a normal business cycle, plans between consumers and producers eventually become uncoupled. In the beginning, producers learn what consumers want. They produce these products, and consumers buy them. After a while, consumers either do not need more of the products, or their tastes change and the products no longer fit their needs. Producers, unaware of a shift in consumers' needs, produce at an accelerated pace. They assume that people who bought three pairs of jeans last year will buy five pairs this year. The unsold stock accumulates as inventory. Producers have more than they can sell. Production is reduced, and workers are laid off. The workers cannot afford to buy the product; their consumption drops, and production is reduced further. Corporations that do not adapt go bankrupt. Companies that fail to innovate may survive but will go into eclipse. In the meantime, entrepreneurs see what consumers need, and they move to produce it, but they must do so at a low cost because conditions are not good. The innovations of the entrepreneurs may be adapted by the existing corporations, or the entrepreneurs may absorb the older companies. Either way, the search process has created new methods and industries, and has destroyed existing businesses that could not adapt. Creative destruction leads to a revival of the business environment.

The much vaunted "productivity revolution" in the United States in the 1980s was a classic example of creative destruction, particularly in the automotive industry. In 1974, there was a crisis. The price of gasoline rose threefold, seemingly overnight. Conservation became the byword. In addition, air pollution was a rising concern. The U.S. Government set standards for emissions. Americans, known for their love affair with cars, wanted energy-efficient vehicles. Detroit manufacturers assumed that whatever they produced would be embraced by the public. "What's good for General Motors is good for the country." They responded with small, cramped, underpowered cars that were inferior to the competing foreign models and were far more expensive.

The competition, of course, came from Japan. The Japanese had automated their production process so they could produce small, high-quality cars. They were cheap and reliable, and they ran well for their size. Detroit went into crisis. Some pundits proclaimed that the United States would no longer be able to compete in the world auto market. Every year, Detroit produced new Gremlins, Vegas, Pacers, and other small cars. They were all lemons. Chrysler had to be bailed out by the federal government in an unprecedented move. Unfortunately, the automobile industry provided a showcase of America's problem. There was widespread pessimism; many Americans believed that the United States could never compete on the assembly line, particularly with the Japanese. Virtually any science fiction movie made in the late 1970s and early 1980s depicted a future dominated by Japanese corporations. The Japanese had specialized in small cars, perceiving a need that Detroit could not fulfill. They found a way to make small, cheap, high-quality cars at low cost, and their innovations changed the automotive industry. The effects of those innovations are still felt today, even as a Japanese economic crisis unfolds in the 1990s.

The U.S. economy spent much of the late 1980s and early 1990s renovating the industrial base to become more competitive. The process seems to have worked, for now. The U.S. economy is presently the healthiest in the world. At this writing, it is unclear whether this is entirely an effect of the productivity gains of the 1990s. Some of the health can be attributed to those elements of renewal, but we may also be seeing a lucky convergence of other factors. Even now, however, uncertainty continues to reign.

UNCERTAINTY AND COMPETITION

At this point, it may be useful to review what we mean by *true uncertainty*. We are in a state of true uncertainty when we cannot know all of the possible consequences of our actions.

Thus, true uncertainty occurs when we are unaware of all the facts or are ignorant of the process as a whole. In a free market, decentralization creates this condition. Each individual, in pursuit of his or her own goals, interprets available information subjectively. None of us can know how everyone else will react to new events or to existing conditions. Our ignorance of how things will change in the future prevents us from predicting how events will unfold in real time. And because we do not know all of the possible outcomes, we are unable to use standard probabilities.

Calculating probabilities requires knowing how often something will happen when current conditions are repeated over and over again. Subjective probabilities, as we discussed in Chapter 2, are a convenient "fudge" factor.

The options available to us when we make a decision are products of real time. Our options are dependent not only on our own past decisions, but also on the past decisions of other participants with whom we may have direct or indirect connections. On a grand scale, many of our options are limited by cultural norms, and these limitations are often temporary and even silly. For instance, in the United States in the 1960s, it was virtually unthinkable for a boy to take flute lessons. The flute was a "sissy" instrument. But then Ian Anderson, a rock musician and musical entrepreneur, made the flute "masculine" by treating it as a phallic symbol on stage. Before John F. Kennedy was elected, having a non-Protestant President was unthinkable. Even in election year 2000, the concept of a female or a minority President is not a realistic option. Economic times can also limit the options open to individuals. When sheer subsistence is the priority, dreams are set aside.

Many of the limits we face are the effects of our own past choices. When a painter begins with a blank canvas, the possibilities are endless. With each brush stroke, however, the possibilities narrow.

In business, a producer is limited not only by economic conditions and available technology, but also by consumer tastes, competitors, and personal perspective. Prices may be set too high because producers believed that others could not charge less for a similar product and still make a profit. Prices that are set too low squeeze the profit margins, and the producers go out of business. Products are often hurried to market in order to cash in on a fad or a trend, but they arrive when the trend is over.

All of these uncertainties lurk in the marketplace because of the imperfect coordination that exists among participants. Each participant shares some of the knowledge, but subjectively interprets the stock of common knowledge. Because of these uncertainties, multiple *simultaneous* searches for a solution are ongoing. This search-and-discovery process, under conditions of true uncertainty in real time, is called competition.

From its inception, the potential of the Internet was apparent. But, remember, the Internet is not the World Wide Web. The Internet is merely a set of protocols that allows computers to communicate with one another. What the computers say, what information is communicated, and how it is presented are all application-specific. When the Internet first came to public prominence, there were bulletin boards, FTP, the Usenet, closed systems (like America Online), and, finally, the World Wide Web. Each approach had its own interpretation as to how the Internet should be used, based on the technology available at the time. The Usenet and bulletin boards were for group discussions that involved posting responses. Rather than occurring in real time, discussions took place in discrete time over a long period. FTP was for downloading information. Closed systems provided graphical environments with prescribed applications. Finally, the World Wide Web offered different sites linked by *hypertext*. Hypertext links are highlighted words that allow users to jump from one site to another without having to type in a new address. Navigating the World Wide Web was difficult until the founders of Netscape produced the first graphical "Web browser." The concept was so successful that most people now consider the World Wide Web the Internet.

Look at what happened here. People saw the potential of the Internet. Useful applications were developed simultaneously. Finally, a solution was chosen: the World Wide Web. The solution is the result of a discovery process motivated by competition, though the goal was not necessarily monetary gain. Indeed, there has long been a movement to keep the Internet commercial-free. Instead, the competition was for fame. The final solution, the Web, not only includes one of the key components of complex systems (loose connections in an open environment), but can also incorporate the other developed areas of the Internet. Through the Web, one can download data via FTP, access newsgroups, and send e-mail. The search process found a solution without a central planner. Creative destruction is also occurring. Bulletin boards are giving way to Web sites. Online chat is slowly replacing the Usenet. On the Internet, competition as a discovery process is happening at an accelerated pace.

Uncertainty was an important element in that development. No one knew which Internet format would work the best. As people chose their paths, based on their skills, resources, and intuition, a solution was found that incorporated much of what people were looking for.

If everyone had known the solution (in the manner of mainstream economics), there would have been no complex search. There would not have been the discovery process that occurred during the search. The discovery process produced unexpected benefits and consequences; among them was the further development of technology as the number of new applications grew. Thus, the discovery process fed back into the hardware development. It also produced a demand for cheap PCs whose primary functions are word processing, household accounting, and access to the Internet, rather than complex, number-intensive applications. These developments could not have been anticipated. In retrospect, the discovery process seems inevitable or even organized, but while it was going on, it seemed disorganized and uncertain. The uncertainty was (and still is) there. The organization was (and still is) too complex for our limited perception.

Chance, which continues to play an important role, enhances our feeling of uncertainty. Yet, the science of statistics allows for a solution to be found even if we do not know where or when it will arrive. *The Economist,* in their August 8, 1992 edition gave us the following example of how statistics are often misunderstood. Everyone knows that when flipping a coin, the chances of getting 6 heads in a row is 0.50 to the 6th power, or 1.5625%. Those are small odds. Yet, if we had a contest where 64 people flipped coins 6 times each, at least one of them would toss six heads in a row with almost 100% probability.

Gina Kolata in the February 27, 1990, issue of *The New York Times* wrote of a real life example. In 1986, a New Jersey resident won the jackpot in the New Jersey lottery twice in 4 months. The odds of any one person accomplishing this feat are staggeringly small, perhaps smaller than 1 in one trillion. Yet, mathematicians have shown that because millions of people play the lottery nationwide, the chances that one of the players win twice in four months condenses to one in thirty, a much more achievable number. These examples show how a multiple parallel search process is more likely to achieve a result even if the chances at the local level (i.e., the individual coin flipper) are quite low. Local randomness and global structure once again emerge. The example also illustrates the difference between the uncertainty we feel as participants and the uncertainty of the process as a whole. The individual coin flippers are all in a high state of uncertainty. No one knows who will win, and their results are truly random. The system, however, knows that *someone* will win, and that is all that matters.

In a complex process, this type of mathematics is used to the system's advantage. The loose links between the participants ensure that each individual has access to the same information, but perhaps not to all of it. Thus, the participants can solve part of the problem and pass the partial solution to others who can build on it. In evolution, this partial transfer can result in a change in species over time. In the economy, we see the evolution of ideas. Each participant has access to information. Some of the participants solve part of a problem. Others continue the work. The more participants who work on the problem, the more likely it is that someone within the system will achieve a final solution. Coordination in a structured way is not as efficient as most people think. Very few direct collaborations result in answers. However, indirect collaborations work well, though they are slower. This is how science and industry work. Many participants contribute to the problem. When enough pieces are worked out, the ultimate solution will finally present itself. Often, the solution shows up in many places almost simultaneously. In science, this process can take centuries. Professor Andrew Wiles's recent solution to Fermat's Last Theorem is linked to the mathematicians of the past. The final solution to the problem originally posed by Fermat around 1637 required 300 years of mathematical development. In the business cycle, time passes faster but works in much the same way.

At the beginning of this chapter, I quoted Louis Pasteur: "Chance favors the prepared mind." Pasteur was pointing to the fact that a combination of luck and skill is usually needed to find solutions, but luck favors those who know how to look. A complex social process works the same way. The parallel search for solutions is much more efficient than a centralized process because more people are looking for the answers. If everyone were searching in isolation, that procedure would be inefficient. The sharing of knowledge increases efficiency dramatically. All we need are enough "threads to buttons" to make the process work. The job of civilization is the open sharing of information, which leads to efficient progress.

As is often the case, there is a downside, or consequence, to the freedom necessary for this kind of development. Being unregulated and decentralized has allowed innovation to occur at an accelerated pace, but unscrupulous and morally questionable applications of Internet technology have occurred. These include familiar problems, from "chain letters" to the fraudulent sale of securities. The question is: What and how much regulation is required to minimize these more unsavory results of the new technology?

The loose connection, the sharing of information and goals, must be maintained while the discovery process remains in place. Uncertainty at this point is usually equated with risk. By leaving uncertainty in the system, we risk the continued growth of unwanted enterprise. On the other hand, putting a rigid structure in place will limit the uncertainty and kill the discovery process. As always, finding the right balance is difficult.

UNCERTAINTY AND CRISIS

It seems obvious that uncertainty reigns during times of crisis. However, crisis itself can be a positive development. It is only negative in that it specifies that change is coming. Most people are uncomfortable with change and equate it with hard times.

Mainstream economics tends to take the same view, calling such events "shocks." They are even referred to as "exogenous"—outside of the system. If it were not for change, according to the mainstream school, everything would continue along in perfect balance, a "circular flow." Change is like an alien invasion. The mainstream view ignores the fact that change is necessary. One of the hallmarks of a process that survives is its ability to adapt to its environment. We know that species that do not adapt become extinct. The same is true of economic and other social systems. Crisis is a signal that change is *needed*. It is not imposed by some outside intelligence. Instead, it is generated from within, to adapt to new developments. In a complex system, this process leads to even greater complexity, which leads to still further adaptability. For instance, the earth's ecosystem has experienced fewer and fewer mass extinctions over time. Developed free-market economies have also experienced fewer and fewer panics on a mass scale. The most recent one, of course, was the worldwide panic of the 1930s. Since then, there have been recessions in the developed world, but nothing like the depression of the 1930s. Change through crisis is different from the innovation that comes from competition. That continuous change, even if it is a creative response, is a regular part of business. A crisis, on the other hand, signals that the process itself needs to change.

The 1930s depression was brought about by excesses in the banking and business system. There was little regulation on lending or on disclosure. Banks and funds were free to sell one practice to consumers, while actually doing another. "Investment trusts" in the 1920s (the ancestors of today's mutual funds) could leverage their portfolios without disclosing the dangers to others. Banks speculated in markets with their depositors' money. Reserve requirements were lax. As long as times were good, no one was concerned. Until the crisis of the

1930s, no real change was accomplished. The change promoted safety and competition. Southeast Asia in the 1990s is facing a similar change brought on by crisis. The result should be the same. As in the 1930s, pain will accompany it, but the change will be for the better.

Crisis is a signal of necessary change. To the Austrian school of economics, it occurs when the participants in an economic system can no longer coordinate their needs and products. In a simple example, the consumers no longer need more of what the producers are making. The producers make too much of their product and then have to lay off workers, which further reduces consumption. When the crisis becomes apparent to everyone, it is usually too late for a remedy. Uncertainty now runs at high levels. We usually think of uncertainty as a consequence of crisis and a sign that the future is unknown where, before, everything was clear. For many observers, this distinguishes "good" times from "bad." In good times, we are optimistic and know where we are headed. Our direction is clear, our prospects are excellent. During crisis, our path is uncertain. We feel we are wandering; we don't know which way to turn. This view is an illusion. Good times generate bad times. If things were really so good during the boom years, we would have seen the problems developing. The seeds of the 1930s depression existed in 1929, whether people knew it or not. It was as though they drove off a cliff because they were not aware that the bridge was out. We all tend to happily drive along until we become aware of a problem. But the problem was always there. Our perspective was just too limited to perceive it.

In bad times, uncertainty is present as a yearning for direction. We know that we are groping for a solution, and that is exactly what is happening. When financial crisis comes, the free market generates multiple searches for solutions. Chance plays a key role in this process. One of the reasons the multiple search process is so efficient is that it increases the chances of a solution being found. As in any complex process, no central planner is involved. During a crisis, there is a large outcry: "Do something about it!" For humans, this means creating a specific plan to address the problem. Yet history has shown that specific plans seldom generate the necessary solutions. This does not mean that the government cannot help the recovery process; it can, but it must do so by changing the environment to promote innovation rather than by generating the innovation itself.

A simple solution has worked in the past: Change the monetary policy. The central bank adjusts interest rates to make the cost of borrowing higher or lower. Why does this work? In good times, easy access to capital does not necessarily promote innovation; instead, it promotes speculation. During good times, there is little need to search for new solutions. Everyone is happy with the way things are. Rather than borrowing money at low rates and using it to develop business, participants use the borrowed funds to speculate in the stock market, real estate, art, or the latest investment fad. In addition, a rapidly expanding economy leads to higher costs because the demand for labor and materials rises when production increases. Thus, a central bank will raise interest rates to keep the economy from "overheating." Speculative and pricing pressures are kept at a minimum. During the crisis, the central bank has a different problem: Pessimism is usually very high. To promote economic growth and innovation, interest rates are reduced. Solvent entrepreneurs and businesses borrow money and search for solutions to the crisis. Monetary policy enhances the *conditions* necessary for economic stability without imposing a particular solution on the free market.

This assumes that other rules are in place to promote competition as well. Unfortunately, there seems to be a misconception that the long-term outcome of an unregulated market is

continuous competition. History has shown otherwise. Unregulated economies lead to monopolies; one company controls an
entire industry. The United States had this problem at the start
of the twentieth century. If industries were again deregulated,
there is no reason to think that the same result would not happen. It appears at the time of this writing that Microsoft has become such a monopoly. In the beginning of the PC market,
many different operating systems were available. (An operating
system—the software that controls a PC's components—is similar to the human autonomous nervous system.) When IBM entered the PC market, it chose Microsoft's MS-DOS operating
system. The IBM architecture, unlike Apple's, was not propri-
etary. As other entrepreneurs began to copy the IBM PCs
they created clones that were "IBM-compatible" and used Microsoft's MS-DOS system. As IBM-compatible systems began
to dominate business, so did the MS-DOS approach. Microsoft
branched out into other software, integrating it more and more
with the Microsoft operating systems. Today, only two operating systems are available, Apple's and Microsoft's (now evolved
into Windows). IBM-compatibles have 95 percent of the PC
market. Consumers have a choice of PC manufacturers, but
they have little choice in operating systems. Now that the Web
browser is integrated with the Windows operating system, consumers automatically receive Microsoft's Web software. They
can easily buy a competitor, like Netscape, but why should they
when Microsoft gives them a comparable browser for "free."
The U.S. Government considers this an example of monopoly
power: The consumer no longer has a choice, and there is little
competition. With almost no competition, Microsoft no longer
has to face an uncertain marketplace, and eventually may have
less incentive to innovate. Eventually, consumers could be stuck
paying a high price for something they are not happy with; still,
they have no choice but to continue buying. Eventually, a crisis

will develop: the needs of consumers and the ability of the software to deliver will no longer mesh. However, there will be no multiple search process because no one will be able to compete with Microsoft. The lack of regulation could result in less competition, and, eventually, a lack of innovation.

Regulation is needed to keep the free market "free." But the purpose of regulation is to promote competition, not to dictate to industry the products that should be developed. Regulation, in conjunction with monetary policy edicts, would allow the search for solutions to continue during a crisis. This is the "creative destruction" described by Joseph Schumpeter. Crisis becomes the sign of a need for change. The process of change may not always be pleasant, but it is necessary. The uncertainty that accompanies a crisis is also necessary. The only way to eliminate uncertainty is to dictate a detailed plan for the future. We have seen again and again that such "planned recoveries" do not work. The Japanese government has been trying for over nine years to dictate such a change. Japanese business, which is used to a structured response coordinated by the central government ("Japan, Inc."), *waits* for instruction rather than searching on its own. As a result, one group is trying to find a solution, rather than many contributors of ideas. The solution for Japan will continue to be elusive as long as this structure remains unchanged.

The former Soviet Union was an even starker example. Its system was unable to change and keep pace with the outside world. The need for protection and the need for production were never balanced properly. The process was centralized. While everyone waited for a solution from the central planning authorities, the situation continued to deteriorate. Soviet citizens had faced little economic uncertainty. They did not have to make many choices themselves. Their system, unable to search on its own for a solution, finally collapsed and became extinct.

The certainty of the Soviet system was unable to cope with the uncertainty created by a changing environment.

ENDOGENOUS CHANGE

In this chapter, we have seen that crisis and competition go hand in hand. They are merely different versions of endogenous change. In a global economy, the only exogenous change would come from a natural disaster, like an earthquake or comet strike, or a political change, like a revolution. Otherwise, change is normal. Continuous change, or innovation, continues at a regular pace; crisis occurs infrequently and results in an overall change in the system. In both instances, uncertainty is a necessary component. The random nature of the multiple search process is the uncertainty we feel. We do not know what the solution will be, or when it will arrive. If we did, there would be a potential for a "riskless" profit, which the system will not allow.

Free markets are thus characterized by feedback, which leads to innovation, and by crisis, which leads to changes in the process itself. These forms of endogenous change are hallmarks of complex systems and point to the relationship between the sciences of complexity and the Austrian school of economics. Spontaneous organization and endogenous change lead to adaptability. There can be nothing static about such a process. The Austrian emphasis on process rather than state is perhaps its greatest contribution.

CHAPTER 8

Economic Evolution:
Change in Real Time

> . . . all economic problems are caused by unforeseen change
> which require adaptation.
>
> —F.A. Hayek

IN the previous chapter, we examined crisis and change as events. Here, we will add the critical dimension of *time*. Whether through gradual adaptation or the abruptness of crisis, change becomes equated with "evolution" once we examine how it occurs through time. Since Darwin, the concept of evolution has permeated any time-dependent process. The popular conception of Darwinian evolution has unfortunately strayed far from the intent of its originator. Misconceptions have spread to economic and social systems even as they tainted the theory of species evolution. The concept of evolution is important; especially significant is the role true uncertainty plays in the understanding of complex processes, including economics. The Austrian school, for instance, ties economic evolution to the concept of "creative destruction," where the economy adapts itself to an unforeseen change—a crisis. In this way, the economy evolves because change is generated *endogenously*. In the mainstream school, change is exogenous. Crisis occurs from without, so there is no evolution. The concept of an *evolving* economy is an important consequence of the subjectivist assumptions of the Austrian school. Thus, evolution becomes a critical area of study in the economics of complexity, as opposed to the static equilibrium economics of the mainstream school. Evolution is so important that, in this chapter, we will examine the topic as it applies to both natural and social processes. To do so, we need to understand what evolution really means and what it does not mean.

GOING BACKWARD

Perhaps the best way to understand how the public defines evolution is by examining its antithesis: "de-evolution." In many television situation comedies and science fiction shows, something de-evolves if it goes backward, to a simpler state. Thus, humans would de-evolve if future generations began to resemble our more simian-looking ancestors. De-evolving further would reduce us to bacteria, and finally to the primordial ooze all life came from.

If de-evolving means going backward in time to a simpler form, then evolving means progressing forward to an ever more complex state. In science fiction, when humans evolve, the advanced form is usually one of pure thought or pure energy. Material bodies are no longer needed. Advanced creatures have "evolved beyond the need for physical bodies"—or so said an Organian, on the original *Star Trek* television series.

Evolution is also accomplished by *survival of the fittest*. The mutated versions of earlier species are replaced with new and improved versions. The older models, now obsolete and unnecessary, cannot compete against them and die out. In Social Darwinism, the same thing occurs. The fittest (i.e., the superior) society replaces the inferior. Thus, in the opinion of Social Darwinists, Native American society, being more primitive, had to be replaced by the technologically superior European version. The Spanish colonists took the same view of the Mayans and Aztecs. Seeing that their culture was technologically superior to Native American culture, the Europeans rationalized that European religion was morally superior as well. Hence, Native Americans had to become Christians or die. Likewise, eighteenth-century Europeans felt that because Africans were clearly primitive, making them slaves was justified. This same rationalization has been used down through the centuries to justify war, genocide, slavery, and bigotry. Thus, evolution became defined as a natural form of competition in which the superior entity wins. Interestingly, the view that evolution represents progress from a simpler to a more complex and superior form through survival of the fittest was not what Darwin proposed. What Darwin did propose, and how it changed in the public imagination, is a fascinating story. It also highlights the Victorian tendency to remove uncertainty from a process. One consequence of the popular view of evolution is that the most crucial element—natural selection—is removed.

Herbert Spencer and Social Darwinism

Darwin did not originally use the phrase *survival of the fittest*. In fact, in the first five editions of *The Origin of Species,* he did not even use the term *evolution.* Instead, he used *natural selection* for the former, and the more obscure *descent with modification* for the latter. When the now-popular terms finally appeared in his book, Darwin had taken them from another person's work—at the insistence of his friend, Alfred Russell Wallace. That person was Herbert Spencer, who in his day was more influential than Darwin when he wrote about social history and analysis.

Spencer equated evolution with "progress." He believed that natural and social systems move from the "homogeneous to the heterogeneous"; that is, they begin with a simple form and become ever more complex as they evolve. With this complexity comes variety. As the present-day ecology evolved from simple bacteria, so did our complex "enlightened" society evolve from its more primitive ancestors. It is easy to see why this belief is so widespread. Most people equate the past with simpler times. Unfortunately, each generation feels this way. Romanticizing the past is a common pastime. The fact that Spencer's ideas became widespread is symptomatic of the Victorians' view that their age was complicated, although we look back on it as slow-moving and "quaint." The concept was also consistent with the Victorian belief that humans were the ultimate goal of evolution. This view was depicted in H.G. Wells's story, "The Island of Dr. Moreau." In the original story, Dr. Moreau surgically modifies animals so that they become physically more like humans. Somehow, they also gain a rudimentary intelligence when they assume a more humanlike shape. Speech merely requires the construction of the appropriate voice box. Dr. Moreau tries to play God by evolving the animals himself to their logical final form: humankind. This causes his own destruction because humans are not allowed to play God.

Wallace's assignment of a role to God persuaded Darwin to use the term *evolution* rather than *natural selection* in later editions of his work. Wallace argued that natural selection implied that there must be a selector—hence, God. Darwin capitulated because he wished to keep his theory as secular as possible.

Unfortunately, Spencer's concept of evolution was contrary to Darwin's. Darwin wrote that natural selection occurs because there is complexity; that is, a variety of species is available to select from. Contrast this with Spencer's belief that variety and complexity were consequences of evolution, not the conditions for it.

More than the theory of evolution, the concept of survival of the fittest has been the source of so much human suffering that it is hard to know where to begin to describe it. The phrase implies that evolution not only is an *efficient* selector, but it also makes *optimal* decisions. Only the fittest, or the *best*, survive. Those who are inferior die out or *should be replaced*. Unfortunately, this concept has little relationship with either Darwinian evolution or what we know to be reality. Even in nature, evolution does not efficiently select or evolve. Our own bodies contain numerous examples of this. Nesse and Williams describe many of these "design flaws" in their book, *Why We Get Sick*. An obvious example is the design of our food conveying and air conveying mechanisms. They are right next to each other, and although a flap of skin is present to stop food from going down our windpipe, it does not always work, and thousands of people die each year from choking on food. Why aren't the two pipes separate from one another? Because our distant ancestors (worms) did not breathe air, but they did take in food through their mouth. Eventually, as air breathing developed, it was more convenient to adapt the mouth and nose for breathing. This necessitated an elegant though imperfect solution that is manifest in our anatomy. It would be different if we could design it from scratch, however.

An even more intriguing example is our appendix—an organ that serves no useful purpose except to "enable us to have appendicitis," as Nesse and Williams say. It has become smaller, but our appendix has shrunk to a long thin form as opposed to the larger version that rabbits have (and still use). At first glance, you might think that the appendix is slowly shrinking away as an effect of evolution. However, a long thin appendix appears less prone to appendicitis than a large round version. Thus, the appendix has evolved into a shape that is less prone to infection. Being less intrusive, it can continue to exist even though it no longer serves a useful purpose. One can only wonder how many social and business institutions have managed to evolve themselves in the same manner.

The idea that nature always makes the best choice is wrong. This misconception has been used to justify slavery, genocide, and numerous other heinous acts of human versus human. It has even been adapted to economics. Particularly in the 1990s, with the success of free-market economies, there is widespread belief that the free market knows what is best. "Let the free market decide" has become a rallying call for those who do not wish to make a decision. Yet, there are numerous instances, even in recent times, where the best product did not win. In the previous chapter, we discussed the Apple Macintosh system's superiority to the Microsoft MS-DOS operating system used on IBM-compatible PCs in the 1980s and early 1990s. As of this writing, Apple has a mere 5 percent of the PC market. Even though Apple was first with the innovation and delivered it in an attractive way, it still lost to its competitor.

An earlier example involved videocassette recorders (VCRs). In the early 1980s, there were two noncompatible systems: VHS and Betamax. Betamax was universally believed to be superior for its quality of image and sound. VHS and Betamax were comparably priced, yet Betamax died. VHS, the acknowledged inferior system, is now the standard video recording format.

These examples refute the idea that the free market picks the best product. The inferior products won for other reasons. In the case of MS-DOS, IBM concentrated on the business market while Apple focused on schools. Unfortunately, if a family is to have one system, and there is a choice between the breadwinner's working at home (which is usually required) or the children's doing computer work at home (which was not required in the 1980s when only the very wealthy could afford a home PC), the breadwinner wins out. The home PC had to be compatible with the one used at work, no matter how much more difficult it was to learn and use. This fed back into the marketplace, and the demand for MS-DOS applications continued to grow.

Feedback also played a role in the victory of VHS over Betamax. In what has now become a standard case study in business schools, VHS did a better job of advertising the system and getting movies produced in the VHS format. Consumers came into video stores, saw how VHS tapes outnumbered Betamax, and bought VHS recorders. Store owners saw that more VHS tapes were being rented, so they stocked more. The cycle continued to expand, and, eventually, Betamax simply faded away.

For both MS-DOS and VHS, more than superiority was involved in survival. It is not necessarily the "best" that survive, so fitness must be defined differently than Herbert Spencer defined it. One thing is clear: the products that survived were not the best, but they were good enough; that is, they satisfied the customers enough so that other considerations came into play when the choice of format was made. In the choice of a VCR, there was no evolution from a simpler to a more complex environment. In the end, the decision became simpler because there was no other choice. In Darwin's theory, natural selection *required* variety so a choice could be made. Variety did not occur as a result of the development of the VCR market.

Perhaps the most important problem with the popular (Spencerian) definition of evolution is that it is not creative. Natural selection implies that the evolutionary process picks a near-optimal solution from a variety of possible solutions. Usually, more than one solution survives. (Apple continues to hold a part of the PC market.) The fact that some choices become extinct implies that the system also tries many solutions, many of which are mistakes, or evolutionary dead ends. This error-making process allows natural selection to take place.

The popular idea that free markets work like a bastardized "efficient" version of Darwinian evolution does not reflect the truth about how markets adapt. In fact, the popularization of such a view gives the public—particularly in developing countries that may have just emerged from a socialist or fascist type of economy—unrealistic expectations as to what a free market can deliver. If the Darwinian concept is in error, what can take its place? Luckily, the sciences of complexity describe experience in a much better fashion.

PROBLEMS WITH DARWIN

As heretical as it may seem, Darwin was essentially wrong. He set us on the right path, but the basic premise of Darwinian evolution has deep flaws.

Suppose you wake up one morning and find that you have lost your car keys. You have no idea where you lost them, but you have an important meeting scheduled and you need to find them quickly. If you search through the house randomly, going from one room to another on a whim, it will take you a long time to find your keys. Admittedly, once in 100 times, you may get lucky and find your keys quickly this way, but most of the time, your search will take forever if you wander aimlessly around the house. Instead, you need a plan. Where do you last remember having the keys? What route did you take from the car to the house? Are your keys in your coat pockets, where you often leave them, or on the floor, below where you deposited your coat? You adopt a number of search plans because you know that a pure random search takes too long. Darwin's theory is much like the pure random search and, for the same reason, it does not work.

Darwin's theory of evolution was based on the concept of gradualism; random mutations cause minor changes to an organism. Mutations that contribute to survival or efficiency are accumulated, over time, by the process of natural selection. Darwin had an example on hand: animal breeders. As we know, wild poodles never roamed the earth. Poodles are the creation of humans who selectively bred dogs over time. Darwin felt that because humans could cause a change in a breed through natural selection, then nature, by selecting random mutations that are useful, could do the same thing over eons of time. Through computer experiments, however, scientists confirm that selection based on random mutations would take too long to account for the current state of Earth's ecosystem.

The following example is taken from *At Home in the Universe,* by Stuart Kauffman. Suppose a simple organism has 1,000 genes. Then, the number of combinations of possible genes is $2^{1,000}$, or 10^{300} (a 10 followed by 300 zeros). Suppose we are going to search through these combinations to find the best one, and we are able to test one of these combinations every billionth of a second. It would still take us 10^{291} seconds to find the best combination. A billion seconds is approximately 257 years, and a billion is 10^9. Literally, 10^{291} seconds is an astronomical length of time. In fact, it is longer than the age of the known universe. When this one change to a relatively simple organism would take longer than time itself, *random* mutation cannot be the selection criterion.

A simple bead game (paraphrased from M. Eigen and R. Winkler's excellent book, *Laws of the Game*) shows us that selection may have nothing to do with "fitness," when based on random selection:

Selection: Variation 1 (Random)

We start with a square playing board with squares like a checker board, measuring about 4 × 4 squares. We have four beads in four colors (16 beads total) which are placed randomly on the board. Then we roll a pair of dice using the numbers as coordinates of the beads (ignore rolls with five or six in them since no such coordinate exists). The chosen bead is taken off the board. The dice are rolled again, and the color of the next bead chosen replaces the bead removed in the previous roll. The current bead is left alone. Thus, the second bead chosen is doubled with the second roll. Eventually the board becomes filled with one color bead, and the game is over.

There is always a winner in this game, but we can never predict who will be selected, though the process certainly "selects" someone. Eigen and Winkler point out that the "fittest" in this game is the winner. There is no other criterion for selection. Thus, natural selection, when randomly applied, will always select someone, but there is no reason for that selection.

Selection: Variation 2 (Mutation)

After the second roll, a "mutation" roll is added. If a number other than "six" is rolled, replacement occurs as in Variation 1. However, if a six is rolled, then the color used for replacement is the one with the fewest beads on the board.

This version never ends. It usually keeps any one color from dominating. Thus, it keeps the search process constantly moving. Mutation does not result in equilibrium, just continual change.

Selection: Variation 3 (Birth and Death)

In the above examples, the birth and death rate was the same for each color bead. Suppose we give one bead an edge:

It has more chances to reproduce than die. When you roll the dice, a third dice is added. For red, if a 1 is rolled, then the bead is replaced. If the number is 1 through 5, then it is doubled in the next roll. Give the other colors varying birth and death rates. Red is the most likely to survive, but not always. While only one color can survive, and red is most likely, the odds are not 100%.

If the mutation effect of Variation 2 is added to Variation 3, red is always selected. Mutation is still random. The colors that are mutated and the sequence of mutation cannot be predicted. Yet, in the end, red always dominates. The addition of a purely random element has somehow tipped the scales more completely toward red. Red is the fittest, but that fact alone is not the answer because, without mutation, red may not dominate. Evidently, a purely random element had to be introduced in order to steer the process to the optimal answer. The question is: "Why?"

GENETIC ALGORITHMS

We tend to think of genetics as the stuff of science fiction. The actual process of selection is unknown, but we are learning more and more. One of the intriguing models of genetic evolution consists of "genetic algorithms." Genetic algorithms mimic the theory of genetics in creating a set of optimal rules. A combination of rules and randomness may explain why Variation 3 with mutation always ends up red, even though the path it takes varies each time.

Genetics describes the way the gene pool combines and recombines to create new living entities. As we know, each person is different, though we all have anatomical similarities. Our basic genetic code determines the fact that our faces consist of two forward-looking eyes, one nose, one mouth, and two ears. The basic form of the human face is the same for our entire species. However, all the faces are different. Our eyes, to take one example, are subject to numerous variations of color, shape, distance apart, and size relative to the rest of our face. However, in all normal cases, two eyes are located in approximately the middle of the face, along a horizontal axis. Our species-related genetics are responsible for the universal similarities in our eyes. However, the mixing of the gene pool in our ancestors is responsible for our eyes' individual characteristics.

The mixing of the gene pool occurs through three methods:

1. A particular genetic trait may die out because all of the carriers of that gene die. For instance, in the northern regions of Europe, blue-eyed people dominate. That is because of the shorter days and colder weather, fair-skinned and light-eyed people have better survival characteristics. In the warmer climates, the opposite seems to be true. Warmer weather and longer days tend to favor those with darker complexions and brown eyes. This runs the gamut from the olive complexions of the Mediterranean regions to the darker skins of Africa. Nonetheless, there appear to be survival characteristics associated with those physical types in those regions. This is the equivalent of "survival of the fittest."

2. Individual characteristics are passed on from generation to generation by the mixing of the characteristics of the parents. This method is called genetic crossover. The result of the mixing depends on the characteristics of the genes themselves. In the case of eye color, we know that the gene for brown eyes *dominates* the *recessive* gene for blue eyes. We all have two genes for eye color. If one parent has two brown-eye genes and the other has two blue-eye genes, the children can either have two brown-eye genes or one brown and one blue. Either way,

all the children will have brown eyes due to the dominant gene. On the other hand, if one parent has two blue-eye genes while the other has one blue eye and one brown eye gene, then the children can either have two blue-eye genes or one of each color. In this case, there is a one-third chance that offspring will have blue eyes even if one parent is brown-eyed. In my own family's case, for instance, I have brown eyes and my wife has blue eyes. Both of our children have blue eyes, so I am clearly carrying a blue-eye gene in my makeup.

3. *Mutation* may occur. Because of science fiction, mutation seems to get a lot of popular press, but mutation is so uncommon and slow moving that, among humans, we hardly ever see it. In mutation, a gene randomly changes into something completely different. The reason for mutation is not really understood. Sometimes it is caused by damage that occurs at morphogenesis. We do know that radiation can cause mutation. Suppose someone was born with purple eyes. If purple eyes dominated both blue and brown eyes, then there is a chance that purple eyes after a number of generations could become another dominant color. On the other hand, if it is recessive, it would probably die within a generation.

Genetic algorithms mimic the mechanics of genetics to optimize a set of rules. The rules used in genetic algorithms are of the if–then type: If A happens, then do B; else do C. An example that immediately comes to mind is how investors pick stocks. Most individuals have a set of criteria for buying and selling stocks. Suppose you have a list of a dozen criteria that you think will help you pick good stocks. A genetic algorithm can be enlisted to select the best combination of six rules. The following example shows how you might go about optimizing the rules. (Those interested in more details should read John Holland's book, *Hidden Order*, or Richard Bauer's *Genetic Algorithms and Investment Strategies,* which goes into specific details for stock selection.)

The process tests all twelve rules over a period of four years and picks the eight rules that produce the most profits. Thus, it eliminates the "weak" rules, and only the most profitable (the fittest) rules survive. Then the process can test unusual combinations of rules by periodically grafting the "if" part of one rule onto the "then" part of another rule. It tests the new rule to see whether it works better than the two "parent" rules used to generate it. If so, one of the parents is dropped and the "offspring" is used; otherwise, the offspring dies. In addition, at a specified low rate, a part of one rule, selected at random, is randomly flipped. This "mutates" the rule into a completely new rule. The equivalent would be a rule like "If yield is higher than 5 percent, then buy." The "buy" part of the rule would be randomly flipped to "sell," and that rule would be tested. This can be particularly interesting if an offspring rule is mutated.

In practice, a series of rules can be effectively optimized using genetic algorithms. Our subject here is not optimal decision making. However, the reason genetic algorithms work illustrates how evolution can, through a structured search process with random elements, find a solution more effectively than other methods.

When we optimize a set of rules, we are usually trying to maximize something. In the above example, it was profits. Profits are calculated by trading off revenues and costs. In an optimization routine, we start with a set of assumptions, calculate the revenues and costs, and then look at the profits. After the initial calculation, we have another go at it by changing the assumptions and recalculating the profits. If the profits under the new assumptions are better than in the previous iteration, the routine continues. The level of profits is like a hill. As profits grow, we continue climbing the hill. After a while, the costs outstrip the revenues, and profits decline. We have crossed the pinnacle of the hill of potential profits and have started down the other side. The optimizer knows where the peak was and pronounces that point the best, or "optimal" solution. However, most problems do not have only one possible solution. Often, several solutions are distantly related to one another. When many hills have potential solutions, the "optimal" solution is the one on the highest peak. Even if our optimization algorithm has reached the peak of the hill we are on, there may be other hills with even higher peaks. But the optimization algorithm will not be aware of these other peaks. All it knows is that it has reached the peak of the hill it is on.

Solving a problem that has multiple solutions is like trying to find the highest peak in a mountain range while blindfolded.

When we know that we are on a multihilled "fitness" land-scape, how do we search? Merely picking a hill at random and saying "that one's good enough" is *not* good enough. On the other hand, we cannot test all of the hills. That would take too

long. So, what do we do? The genetic algorithm, like other optimization processes, also climbs a hill. However, the crossover
and mutation functions periodically throw the optimizer off of
the hill we are on and test another hill (or a different set of
rules) by *creating* new rules. If the new hill is not as high as the
original one, we will eventually climb off the new one and go
back to the original one by eliminating the new rule. On the
other hand, if the new hill has higher "fitness" than the old one,
we will stay on it. Thus, the genetic algorithm systematically
searches the fitness landscape to find the highest hill in the
mountain range. The search process can be ended by reaching a
certain tolerance (where we decide that a result is close enough)
or by running out of time. Either way, when the algorithm generates an adequate level of fitness, it will stop. Finding *the* optimal solution is then unnecessary.

Let's look at what is happening within a genetic algorithm.
The search for the best set of rules, based on the initial list, is
pretty straightforward. The most fit survive; those that are
weaker are eliminated. However, we do not need any fancy
gear to look for that outcome. In addition, there is some random "mating" of rules to produce new rules. Some of the new
rules are better than those that produced them. The weaker
ones are eliminated, and the stronger ones replace the parents.
However, the generation of these rules is strictly random.
There is no way to know which ones will work, or even what
they will be. Remember, there will be several generations of
these rules. The final optimal offspring may bear little resem-
blance to the initial rules. Finally, there are mutations, which
again happen at random. When combined, these random elements make the search process more concise while simultaneously creating new possibilities.

Rather than randomly searching the fitness landscape for
the highest peak, the genetic algorithm searches for it in a

structured manner. The results are much closer to those that we see in the history of real species. With genetic algorithms, we can see how a process can evolve in a shorter sequence of time. A complex process will search in a structured manner; it will not conduct a random search by mutation alone.

Randomness is an important element in the process. Once again, innovation and growth do not emerge through planning, but through a combination of randomness and structure. The structure is in the search process itself. The randomness is in the way the various rules are transformed and tried. Thus, the creativity of the genetic algorithm methodology comes from random elements. We cannot predict what path the genetic algorithm will take in its search for a solution, just as we cannot be sure what solution will be found. There is no plan, no path that must be followed. In fact, there are multiple potential paths, but they lead to the same basic vicinity. In looking at evolution, the result seems inevitable. That is why the Victorians assumed that progress must be the result of evolution. Instead, we see a search for solutions and the creation of possibilities. Finding the optimal solution would take too long. However, a near-optimal solution can be found. Exactly what it is cannot be predicted.

Is it perfect? No. Sometimes the fitness landscape is so complicated that *the* optimal solution can never be found. On the other hand, a *good* solution will be found. The ending solution depends on some interesting factors. First are the basic rules themselves—the "genetic material," if you will. The second factor is the sequence of rule matings (crossovers) and mutations that occur. The third factor is the path that these random events lead to. This characteristic brings us back to the first lines of this chapter. Time, or the sequence of change, is important. That a usable solution will be found is fairly certain. The structure of the actual solution is unknown; it depends on how the random elements combine in real time. The possible combinations are so numerous that we could not list them in advance. Thus, the probability that any one solution will occur is unknown.

Finally, genetic algorithms are creative. When applied to known problems, genetic algorithms not only converge to the known solutions, but may also come up with their own. For instance, John Holland, the father of genetic algorithms, applied the method to solve the Prisoner's Dilemma, a well-known example in game theory. The dilemma is this: Two criminals are captured. They are questioned separately. There is enough evidence to put each in jail for two years. However, if either implicates the other on a greater charge, then he will go free and the other will be put in jail for 10 years. If each implicates the other, then each will get five years. The dilemma facing each prisoner is: "Do I stay mum, or defect? If I defect and the other prisoner does not, he gets 10 years and I go free. If he defects and I do not, he goes free and I get 10 years. If neither of us defects, then we both get two years. If we both defect, we both get five years." Game theorists have found that the optimal decision is to defect. Because the Prisoner's Dilemma can be translated into other types of brinkmanship, such as labor negotiations or arms races, this result is somewhat disheartening. The game can also be played in a series of rounds. Each player knows what another player did in the previous round. In this version, which resembles an arms race, the optimal strategy is called Tit for Tat. It starts like an ordinary Prisoner's Dilemma; the rule is: always defect. After that hurdle, each player always does what his or her counterpart does. Tit for Tat.

John Holland's genetic algorithm also found Tit for Tat to be the optimal solution, but it added its own variation. Remember the simple poker game in Chapter 2? The way to tilt the odds in your favor was to bluff. The genetic algorithm found that the optimal strategy was to try bluffing first. If that does not work, then do Tit for Tat.

Thus, by combining randomness with structure, the genetic algorithm creates an efficient way not only to search for solutions, but also to creatively find new ones as well.

ECONOMIC EVOLUTION

To a large extent, a complex process evolves in the manner of the genetic algorithm. When crisis occurs, the process begins to search for a solution. The solution then becomes part of the process, and the process is changed forever. Thus, change over time becomes evolution. Unfortunately, there is no guarantee that change means progress. In our modern society, for instance, there are many who believe that progress has reduced the quality of life in order to produce more quantity. When a crisis occurs, there is a deterioration in quality and quantity, but the exact nature of this process has been the subject of much debate.

The mainstream school does not really deal with change in the economy. Mainstream economic theory focuses on static quantities and relationships that remain fixed forever. For instance, supply and demand have an inverse relationship. The less there is of something, the more it is in demand and the higher its price. A speculative phenomenon of the 1990s has been Beanie Babies, or "Beanies," which began as small bean-bag animals for children. The animals retail for $4.99. Each animal has a name and a birth date. The TY Toy Company, which produces the animals, periodically stops making specific "retiring" Beanies. The supply of certain Beanies then becomes fixed. Adults began to notice that the prices on some of these retired Beanies were rising as they became scarce and children still wanted them. Early in the Beanies craze, I remember seeing a dinosaur that had been retired. Its price was $35. I considered that amount outrageous and did not buy. Within two years, the dinosaur was selling for $350. Prices of other animals have since risen into the thousands of dollars. This is a classic example of how supply and demand affect prices.

The Beanie Babies example seems to illustrate the power of the mainstream school, but the market for the Beanies does not exhibit the complexity of the full economy. The mainstream school can model specific examples, but it cannot model how the market changes over time.

The Austrian school specifically deals with the evolution of economic *systems,* and, in doing so, it combines all of the elements we have been looking at so far. The Austrian school bases the evolutionary nature of the economy on the subjective tastes and individual objectives of the people who compose the economy. In the normal state of business, the participants are working toward their individual goals. However, the loose connection that participants have through overlapping knowledge and goals leads to the spontaneous organization that characterizes a free-market economy. Each business cycle ends with a crisis. Entrepreneurs work out the solution to the crisis and begin to run their businesses alongside practitioners who are using an older paradigm. Thus, a new business cycle begins. Eventually, the older businesses adapt to the new method, or lose market share and perhaps fade away. The entrepreneurs become the establishment. When a new crisis develops, the cycle starts over again. Crucial to the Austrian school is the notion that the entrepreneurs emerge from the spontaneous organization and are searching for solutions. The entrepreneurs are from within the system, not from outside it.

Until the 1970s, reports, letters, and similar written communications were prepared using a typewriter. Large corporations had groups of people (usually young women) whose sole duty was to type letters and reports for executives. Those of us who are old enough remember what it was like to type a report. Each draft had to be retyped from the beginning. If a typographical error was found, a whole page, or even a series of pages, might have had to be retyped. Any lengthy typing chore was very frustrating. In corporations, pools of typists did this work for executives. Then, in the 1970s, An Wang invented the word processor. Wang's system was an electronic workstation tied into a central minicomputer. For the first time, letters could be "saved" electronically and modified without retyping the entire document. Wang Corporation became a growth company. It went public and became a high-flying stock. In the late 1970s, Wang came to one corporation that had installed his system. The typists gave him a standing ovation as he walked among them. "See," he said, "I have freed them from their typewriters."

However, the system still had problems. It was expensive. It required extensive training, a lot of hardware, and, still, secretaries. When personal computers came to market, one of their first applications was word processing. Microsoft and Lotus, for instance, developed word-processing programs that could run on PCs; a centralized hardware system was no longer needed. In fact, neither was the typing pool. Executives could type and revise their own documents. The PC was cheaper and faster, and no extra personnel were needed. Wang did not adapt. Wang systems continued to be used and purchased as the PC market grew and the software became more sophisticated. However, unable to adapt, Wang went into bankruptcy and now exists as a software firm.

The uncertainty of the competitive environment generates this kind of creativity and opportunity. Entrepreneurs accept the uncertainty that comes with innovation. In many cases, they will say: "We succeeded because we didn't know that the task was impossible." Often, they do not make specific plans or construct a time frame for succeeding. Instead, they plan for the short term and set vague goals for the long term. The goals are often stated as principles, and these are what drive the entrepreneurs. Their goals are the global structure of entrepreneurship. The details of achieving the goals are left flexible. They get woven into the randomness of short-term events. But the global objectives, kept purposely vague, are always there. They lead to the creative response needed by entrepreneurs. In Chapter 9, we will discuss the creative process in more detail. For now, we can say that the entrepreneurs' ability to live with uncertainty is what gives them the incentive to innovate and to persist in their goals.

Uncertainty is a necessary ingredient. In the genetic algorithm, we saw that randomness can lead a process to a goal even when the path remains unknown. This element exists for a good reason: Short-term events are unpredictable. A process that is purely deterministic will not be able to adapt if something unexpected happens. In real life, it is impossible to plan for all the things that might happen, which is why we cannot assess the probability of success or failure of any one action. To survive, a complex process must be able to achieve a goal by multiple means. It will always choose a solution. The solution may not be optimal, but it will be good enough. To find an optimal solution, a complex process must be able to efficiently search the fitness landscape for the highest hill it can find. Random events make the search both efficient and creative. In a free-market economy, then, uncertainty is a necessary element. Only when the economy is in a state of uncertainty can the participants efficiently search for solutions to problems and find creative answers. In addition, only a system that depends on uncertainty can survive unexpected shocks. A complex process can take multiple paths to an optimal solution. It does not require "ideal" conditions; in fact, shocks often force it to find a better solution, a higher hill in the fitness landscape. The "creative destruction" identified by the Austrian school suggests that a free-market economy is not only resilient to shocks, but is also creative and capable of generating innovation. It can only do so while in a high state of uncertainty.

Thus, uncertainty is a necessary condition for complexity and for the functioning of a free market. Without uncertainty, a free market could not innovate and adapt. However, uncertainty also generates loss and hardship. It is the price free markets pay for their resilience and adaptability.

Given the reliance of the Austrian school on the entrepreneur and the importance of the creative function, what are the conditions for creativity? In the next chapter, we will examine the creative impulse for both individuals and the economy. As expected, uncertainty and the ability to live in a condition of uncertainty are critical to the creative function.

CHAPTER 9

Creativity: Uncertainty, Innovation, and Entrepreneurs

I think and think for months and years. Ninety-nine times, the conclusion is false. The hundredth time I am right.
—Albert Einstein

Computers are useless—all they can give you are answers.
—Pablo Picasso

THIS book is primarily concerned with the need for uncertainty in complex processes—particularly, the role uncertainty plays in the ability to *innovate* and to *adapt*. These two attributes are crucial to the ability to learn and evolve. The Austrian economists assigned the crucial role of *economic* innovation to entrepreneurs. In the sense of evolution, the entrepreneur searches for solutions to economic problems and gives the free-market economy its adaptive and evolutionary nature. Often, these solutions are independently discovered by many people. Thus, the PC industry was not developed only by the founders of Microsoft and Apple, but by many others who worked on alternative forms for the personal computer. In the natural sciences, innovations like the calculus were developed independently by two individuals: Sir Isaac Newton and Gottfried Leibniz. Evolution, as we have already discussed, was also developed independently by Charles Darwin and Alfred Russell Wallace. The complex nature of Western society allowed multiple searches, and solutions did not depend on one individual. Up to this point, we have seen that the introduction of uncertainty into a complex process allows an efficient search for a solution, and evolution into a new form that adapts to changes in the environment. In these two cases, society does not depend on any one individual to deliver innovation. Many search, and a few succeed. Society could diversify its efforts, but the ability to deliver results is always uncertain.

Ironically, the creative act itself requires uncertainty in order to exist. Creative people, whether they are writers, artists, scientists, or entrepreneurs, need to exist in a state of uncertainty in order to promote the creative process. In fact, one characteristic that separates creative people, particularly innovators, from the rest of us is their ability to work on a problem for years without knowing whether a solution actually exists. Their challenge may be a scientific problem (Andrew Wiles spent 10 years proving Fermat's Last Theorem) or the development of a personal style of painting or a unique voice in poetry. In their monograph *Art and Fear,* David Bayles and Ted Orland wrote:

> Simply put, making art is chancy—it doesn't mix well with predictability. Uncertainty is the essential, inevitable and all-pervasive companion to your desire to make art. And tolerance for uncertainty is the prerequisite to succeeding.

Interestingly, the source of innovation on a large scale, whether cultural or economic, is similar to creativity at the individual level. Because Austrian economic theory depends on the subjective interpretation of individuals, it will be useful to study creativity at this micro level. The creative process is, in fact, another example of complexity in action. Like other complex processes, uncertainty is a crucial element. Without uncertainty, there can be no creativity.

DEFINING CREATIVITY

How do we define a creative act? Creativity is a process of *integration*, or the merging of previously unrelated items into a new whole. The total is more than the sum of its parts. For instance, Picasso did a sculpture of a gorilla in which the head was two toy Volkswagens with their undercarriages glued together. By changing the nature of the toy Volkswagens, Picasso created an entirely new entity. To prove Fermat's Last Theorem, Andrew Wiles drew together the previously unrelated mathematical fields of elliptic curves and Galois theory. Genius is the ability to see relationships between unrelated items and to integrate them. Innovative genius is the ability to persist in the creative process for long periods of time, exploring many different combinations of what is known, and accepting the definite possibility that nothing of value may result. The ability to live with the uncertainty of the creative process, and persist anyway, sets the innovator apart from someone who merely has good ideas.

Creativity is a *process*. It is not a state or a result. A good deal of myth is attached to creative acts. Artists in particular are prone to promulgating myth. Salvadore Dali said that his genius flowed onto his surrealist canvases. When asked why the Beatles were so popular, John Lennon is reported to have said,

"I wish I knew. Then we could bottle it and sell it." There is a general feeling that true creativity cannot be explained even by the creative people themselves.

Yet, we have many documented instances of creative acts in progress. What is biography but an attempt to explain how an insignificant patent clerk named Albert Einstein could solve the problem of relativity? A truly creative person is one who searches for answers to either concrete or artistic questions. The objectives of the search may vary, but the *process* is similar.

The creative process requires integration of two seemingly contrary processes:

1. The overall goal is known in advance.
2. The method for achieving the goal can take multiple paths or forms.

In an artistic piece, the overall goal is usually referred to as the "theme." The theme can be an expression of feeling, as in Edvard Munch's famous painting *The Scream,* in which a ghostly figure on a bridge is holding its head and screaming to express frustration and anxiety. The theme can also be political. Picasso's mural *Guernica* depicts a single event to express the horrors of war. Often, an artistic goal can be abstract, offering simply a pleasing arrangement of unrelated colors. In science, the goal can be proof of a conjecture that has already been laid down, as with Andrew Wiles and Fermat's Last Theorem. An intuitive feeling can also be a goal. Einstein's insight that gravity and motion may be related led to his proof of General Relativity. Whether the creative process is artistic or scientific, the goal—or theme or theory—gives the process structure. It defines where the creative energy is going to be spent.

The actual method for achieving the goal can take as many paths and forms as there are creative individuals to express them. Many people have painted pictures about the horrors of war, but only Picasso could have created *Guernica.* The details of the creative process cannot be predicted in advance. Creative individuals cannot describe the exact path they will take to achieve their goal. But they can tell you the goal. David Bowie, the rock star, started Glitter Rock in the 1970s. He has said that when he started, he wanted to merge theater with rock and roll, but he was not sure how he was going to do it. The result was Ziggy Stardust, a character that Bowie portrayed while performing rock songs that represented the decadence of the 1970s. He had tried other methods, such as individual story songs, but with the creation of Ziggy Stardust, he achieved his goal.

All along, we have said that complexity is the integration of global structure and local randomness. The creative process integrates the overall goal, which gives the process its structure, with the randomness of the actual search for a solution. The tension between these two elements creates uncertainty, and the uncertainty keeps the creative process searching for a solution. The uncertainty is relieved when the solution is found. In some cases, it is never relieved. After his 1915 paper on General Relativity was published, Einstein devoted his life to developing a Unified Field Theory that would combine molecular, gravitational, and electrical fields. He never found an answer, though he worked on the problem even as he lay on his deathbed. The problem remains unsolved.

In art, an integration of structure and randomness is exemplified by the abstract expressionism of Jackson Pollock. In his "splatter" painting technique, Pollock literally threw paint at a canvas. An unprepared viewer might see merely chaos and randomness. However, by looking at his canvases side by side, viewers can see that Pollock did control the "feel" of each painting. The actual placement of paint was random, but the randomness was controlled. Pollock never lost sight of his goal for each painting, but, unlike traditional painting in which each brush stroke is controlled by the artist, Pollock let fate and gravity determine the placement of specific drops of paint. The result is chaos, but controlled chaos. Pollock was willing to live with the uncertainty that each painting would have elements beyond his control.

A more recent example is the science fiction television show *Babylon 5*. Unlike other TV series, *Babylon 5* was planned as a five-season story. The creator, J. Michael Strazynski (JMS), envisioned a five-year story "arc" around which other, shorter stories could evolve. However, every script had to fit into the larger story, which JMS insisted had a beginning, a middle, and an end. JMS started with a basic outline that revealed some details about the story arc. However, many of the actual details were left to the actual writing. Given the nature of network TV, the show was subject to real-life problems such as technological limitations and actors who did not work out. For instance, the major character of the first season was dropped, and a new main character was introduced in the second season—all without disrupting the main story line. JMS had to stay flexible because the whole project was a work in progress. Like Charles Dickens, who published most of his work in serial form in magazines, JMS was unable to go back and rewrite the plot if a change was needed. Instead, he had to accommodate that change in all the subsequent scripts. The challenge for JMS was to keep the story flexible enough to accommodate the day-to-day problems of running a TV show within a long-term story line. He was able to do that by keeping the global structure (the five-year story line) in mind even as he coped with the local uncertainty of TV production.

In business, an entrepreneur has an idea for a business, stakes his or her financial future on it, and works long hours, sometimes for years, to realize a dream that usually involves more than just making big bucks. Like artistic or scientific innovators, economic innovators do not know, during long periods of work, whether their idea will ever pay off, or even what final form it will take.

It takes a special kind of individual to be able to live with such uncertainty, whether in art, science, or economics. Let's examine the characteristics of truly creative people.

THE CREATIVE INDIVIDUAL

Mihaly Csikszentmihalyi (MC) has written extensively about the creative process and creative individuals. Central to his work is the concept of *flow,* which, despite its name, is a valid area of academic study. Flow refers to a point of optimal achievement, a moment when consciousness and activity become perfectly meshed. A bowler releases a ball and *knows* that it is a strike. A golfer chips out of the rough and knows the ball is going into the cup. A downhill skier reaches championship speed and hits all of the marks perfectly. A writer effortlessly finds the exact words that bring a concept to life. To MC, these are moments when time becomes suspended. A Zen Buddhist would say it is when we become "one" with our activity. As mystical as that may sound, the phenomenon is well documented in MC's books and numerous academic studies. A creative person makes flow—optimal achievement—a normal part of his or her life.

MC's extensive study of creative individuals is described in his book, *Creativity.* An important element that I wish to emphasize is the dichotomous nature of most of his descriptive characteristics. I regard the dichotomy as the tension between global structure and local randomness. This tension breeds the uncertainty that is necessary for creativity to exist.

Three Traits of Creative People

1. Creative individuals use both divergent and convergent thinking. Convergent thinking is "IQ" smarts: the ability to solve problems that have one right answer. Generally, such problems require rational thinking. Divergent problems usually have no single right answer. The quest for a personal artistic style, for instance, is just such a problem. Recall Picasso's complaint about computers, quoted at the start of this chapter. Divergent thinking gives individuals the ability to work on problems that have multiple solutions. A creative individual can use divergent thinking to come up with many solutions, but can then use convergent thinking to pick the right solution out of so many. Thus, a writer can summon many metaphors for the concept of despair, but can also choose the right one for the mood and theme of a particular story. The mood, of course, is the global structure used to judge the appropriateness of all the possible solutions.

An ability to choose among multiple solutions in an almost intuitive manner is what often separates truly creative people from those who only aspire to creativity. A struggle that allows for mistakes is a necessary component of the creative process. People who cannot learn from their mistakes never achieve true creativity. Bayles and Orland, in *Art and Fear*, offered this advice:

> What's really needed is nothing more than a broad sense of what you are looking for, some strategy for how to find it and an overriding willingness to embrace mistakes and surprises along the way. (p. 21)

2. Another paradox is that a creative person needs a combination of playfulness and discipline. Playfulness refers to the ability to throw around all sorts of ideas, no matter how crazy they sound. Many people have great ideas all the time. Why do

we hear from only a handful? Because a truly creative achiever also has discipline—a dogged persistence to carry through an idea, a study, or a novel to the end. Playfulness, which provides the search process for ideas, is often truly random. Discipline gives structure and ensures that the work is actually done.

3. Creative people are able to combine fantasy with a clear sense of reality—to let their imagination run. They can "see things that never were, and ask, 'Why not?'" to quote Robert Kennedy. However, the power of the imagination is useless if it is not grounded in a strong sense of reality. Even the most fantastic work of fiction is useless if it does not tell us something of the human condition in our own reality. In *Gulliver's Travels*, Jonathan Swift satirized and commented on the absurdity of eighteenth-century British law. Even a light fantasy such as the *Star Wars* trilogy is a classic coming-of-age story.

Literature allows us to see how the integration of fantasy and reality lead to a creative act. Perhaps more subtly, structured activities such as art, musical composition, science, and mathematics follow the same path.

Einstein's "Thought Experiments"

In science, the most famous and well documented representative of the ability to integrate imagination and reality was Albert Einstein. There is often a misconception that breakthroughs in mathematics and physics come from manipulating formulas and performing experiments. Those functions are important, but many important discoveries have a different genesis. Einstein performed what he called "thought experiments" to arrive at his ideas. He would imagine an experiment and carry it through, in his mind, to its logical conclusion or implication. His theory of General Relativity (1915) came from a thought experiment that dated from a few years earlier. General

Relativity came from a need to explain how light can be deflected by gravity. In his thought experiment, Einstein imagined himself floating inside a motionless spaceship. Then he imagined that the engines of the spaceship had been turned on. The movement would push him to the floor so that he would be held down by the momentum of the ship. Would he then feel like the ship had gravity? If so, was there a relationship between momentum and gravity? Newton had shown that gravity was related to mass. This new possibility would imply that there was also a relationship among momentum, mass, and gravity. Einstein worked on this idea for over five years, expressing mathematically the insight he gained from his thought experiment. Eventually, he proved that sufficient mass can change the curve of space–time so that even light would be deflected by a large enough mass.

By imagining himself floating in a spaceship, Einstein was
able to see the relationship among momentum, mass, and gravity.

Reexamine what Einstein did. In 1910, humans had barely learned how to fly, let alone think seriously about space travel. Yet, by imagining the stuff of science fiction, Einstein was able to solve a problem that increased humans' understanding of reality by an exponential magnitude.

Imagination integrated with reality leads to innovation. Only by letting their imagination run free can innovators create revolutions. However, only by keeping grounded in reality can true innovation become useful. Imagination is a random search process. It is the ability to examine many possibilities, most of which will not result in anything. Only when it is structured by reality can imagination produce results.

The uncertainty in this search process is the "torture" of a creative life. A creative person will search for a solution that can never be found, for, as Bayles and Orland say, "In making art you court the unknown." MC lists a number of other characteristics of creative people. They all deal with dichotomies. The three characteristics described above point out that uncertainty is a crucial element in the creative process, and the ability to live with uncertainty sets an innovator apart from someone who only comes up with good ideas.

THE CREATIVE PROCESS

The creative process is often described as having five steps:

1. Preparation.
2. Incubation.
3. Inspiration.
4. Evaluation.
5. Elaboration.

This book is primarily concerned with the need for uncertainty in complex processes. Step 2 is therefore the only one that is directly related to our thesis. However, to fully appreciate the role of uncertainty, it is important to understand the entire process. Therefore, I will elaborate on the process here, but with a special orientation toward complex systems and, specifically, toward evaluating creativity as a complex process.

Preparation

The preparation step, which usually takes years, is accomplished without anyone knowing. Specifically, the innovator is internalizing the knowledge and rules of the domain under study. Everyone entering a field goes through this step, but not everyone goes on to those that follow. In the arts, this step amounts to learning the technique or craft involved. Many people with good crafts skills never make great artists. A person with good technique, however, can make a good living. As Bayles and Orland say, "Craft is the visible edge of art."

In the sciences, this step amounts to learning and appreciating the achievements of the past. As the solving of Fermat's Last Theorem showed, scientists do "stand on the shoulders of giants," as Newton said. Any accomplishment builds on the accomplishments of others. Among the contradictory traits that MC listed for creative individuals were "humbleness and pride." Innovators are particularly proud of their work, but they also realize that they are only a point in a long line of change.

During preparation, innovators become intrigued by the unresolved problems of their field. In the physical sciences, they note places where conventional theory does not appear to fully fit reality, such as the dark matter problem discussed in Chapter 4. In the arts, the problem may be expression. For instance, the impressionist painters were specifically trying to discover how they could capture the fleeting nature of light in a static painting. The problem presents itself when the known rules of the domain under study are internalized. This relates to complexity because rules are a crucial component of a complex system. We will address this relationship again later.

The problems themselves appear to fall into two categories. In the first category are known problems—for example, the dark matter problem. Scientists know that there is not enough visible mass in the universe to account for gravity. As they search for a solution, dark matter is one possible answer. In the second category are problems discovered by the innovators. Creation of a new style of painting would fall into this category.

After the problems are identified, the innovators search for solutions. This is where the myth starts.

Incubation

Does inspiration just "hit" someone? Reliable documentation says that rarely happens. Instead, there is a (usually) long period of incubation in which the problem is mulled around, probably by the subconscious. To many observers, this looks like unproductive, idle time. However, creative individuals know that most of their creative work is done in this quiet time. Freeman Dyson, a physicist, said that he was "not ashamed of being idle" and that busy people are "generally not creative."

The arts have a similar process. The following quote, attributed to Mozart, expresses the creative sentiment:

> When I am, as it were, completely myself, entirely alone, and of good cheer—say, traveling in a carriage, or walking after a good meal, or during the night when I cannot sleep; it is on such occasions that my ideas flow best and most abundantly. *Whence* and *how* they come, I know not; nor can I force them.

The incubation phase of creativity is not well understood, and there are many competing theories on how it works. The cognitive psychologists assume that processing is occurring at the subconscious level. The mind is meandering from solution to solution, finding and keeping elements it likes, and discarding those that are not useful. The search for a solution is done through parallel processing; that is, a simultaneous search for solutions goes on. Eventually, the strongest ideas emerge into the conscious mind. This description of incubation is very similar to the genetic algorithm we explored in Chapter 8. It implies that a random element is important to the creative process. Indeed, most help books on creativity offer games that allow individuals to randomly explore ideas. Brainstorming is the most widely accepted manner of doing this in groups.

Incubation is *the* crucial step in the creative process. It is also the step that needs structure even as it generates uncertainty. First, there is the search process itself, which depends on the random testing of ideas in the manner of a genetic algorithm. The search goes on in this manner because it is an efficient method for finding a solution. Often, people think that a plan is needed to solve problems. If the problem is a "presented" problem, then a plan is often useful. However, if it is a "discovered" problem, or one that may not have a solution, then a plan can cause more harm than good. For, as Mozart said, in such problems, a solution cannot be forced. Creative persons must accept that a long period will be spent searching for a solution. They must accept the uncertainty that accompanies the creative process, and acknowledge that it is a crucial part of that process. In essence, uncertainty is necessary in order to be creative, and, for truly creative people, that means living with uncertainty. What often sets innovators apart from other competent people in their fields is their willingness to live with the uncertainty of the creative process. Most people give up, but innovators are persistent. For ten years, in isolation, Andrew Wiles worked on a problem that was deemed, by most people, to be impossible to solve.

Inspiration

The television show *Nova* documented Wiles's achievement. At the beginning of the show, Wiles sat at his desk and described the moment when the final piece of the puzzle of Fermat's Last Theorem came to him. Wiles had already presented a solution, but a flaw was found. It had begun to look like the problem was insurmountable. After a long period of incubation, the final solution presented itself. Wiles tried to describe, for the video audience, the moment when the solution presented itself, but he became so overcome with emotion that he could not continue. Anyone who considers science an exercise in pure logic should see that videotape. It shows the powerful effect of the "Aha!" moment on the creative individual.

Inspiration, the moment of the final solution, gets the most press, but it is the result of the incubation period.

Evaluation and Elaboration

Once insight arrives, it must be evaluated. The late Dr. Richard Crowell used to tell me: "Clever ideas are either incredibly brilliant or incredibly stupid." The last step in the creative process involves evaluating an idea to see whether it really is good, and then elaborating on it so others can understand it. For many creative individuals, elaboration is the most tedious part of the whole process. Alfred Hitchcock was famous for planning the camera angles for his movies before the filming began. He used to say that shooting the actual movie was boring. For many mathematicians and scientists, writing a reportorial book or paper is a tedious affair. Darwin quickly wrote *Origin of the Species* after putting off the chore for several years. Wallace had presented similar ideas, and Darwin was afraid he would not receive proper credit.

The reluctance of many creative people to do the final work related to their discovery or innovation shows, among other things, that the creative *process* is the enjoyable element—more than the actual result or perhaps even the fame, though that is nice too. There is a scene in the movie *Julia* where Dashiell Hammett and Lillian Hellman are talking about fame. Hellman asks Hammett how he handles being famous. Hammett replies, "Fame is just fame. It has nothing to do with writing."

ENTREPRENEURS

As we have seen, the Austrian view of the economic cycle places heavy emphasis on the role of the entrepreneur. Entrepreneurs are the source of creativity. However, entrepreneurs, according to Joseph Schumpeter, do not necessarily have to be individuals. The role of the entrepreneur can be filled by a group, perhaps even a corporation. The entrepreneurial function consists of "doing things that are not generally done in the ordinary course of business routine." Thus, the entrepreneur may be the person who actually does something new, but an entrepreneur can also be someone who influences the way others go about their business.

The composer Charles Ives (1874–1954) has two major accomplishments to his credit. First, he is still well known as a great (perhaps *the* great) American composer. Most of his work was unplayed and unpublished in his lifetime, but it anticipated many twentieth-century innovations, such as twelve-tone music. Second, in his day-to-day work as an insurance company executive, he is widely credited with creating the modern concept of estate planning that is now the mainstay of the insurance business.

Ives was highly influential in changing the way insurance companies functioned, but his work in this area is largely forgotten. As a composer, he stands as a titan, but his work was published so late that he was largely without influence. He has been described as a composer who was "uninfluenced and without influence." So, in his business dealings as an insurance executive, Charles Ives represents the entrepreneurial function of innovation. Although he was an innovator as a composer too, he did not fulfill an entrepreneurial function because he was without influence in the field of music.

An entrepreneur, then, changes the way that business is done, usually in response to a crisis. The question is: Does the cycle of innovation in the economy have a relationship to the creative cycle of individuals? The answer is *Yes*. The economy, according to the Austrians, is an evolving system. Schumpeter said that "static capitalism . . . is a contradiction in terms." An evolving system learns in real time. When a crisis arises, it is similar to the recognition of a problem in the creative cycle. This is followed by an incubation period in which the system searches for a solution. However, no one person is in charge of this search, so there is no organized indication that it is going on. It is, in fact, part of the subconscious of the economy. At some point, an entrepreneur, or several entrepreneurs, come up with a solution, and there is an "Aha!" moment. This is followed by a period of evaluation and elaboration while the free market sorts through the potential solutions and chooses the winners. This is, of course, the basis of competition. The VHS vs. Betamax and the Apple vs. MS-DOS competitions are but two examples.

During this process, the individual participants are not aware that the search is going on or that there will be an outcome. The level of uncertainty for the individual participants is high. In addition, there is no way to eliminate this uncertainty without destroying the process itself. Having a committee choose the "best" product will remove the competitive element—the incentive for the search process to begin with. Instead, uncertainty is such an important part of the process that it is *necessary.* Creativity cannot exist without uncertainty. Innovation in the economy is just as dependent. The uncertainty that the individual elements in the economy face is not the same as risk, though entrepreneurs may face risk as well. This is true uncertainty; even the possible outcomes cannot be known in advance. The final solution can be one of many *near*-optimal solutions. So, even knowing which solution is "best" will not necessarily reveal which solution will win. Winning depends on luck as much as innovation. But the uncertainty generated by competition results in the multiple solutions that the free market can choose from. Eliminate the uncertainty and competition is eliminated. An economic system without competition is not a free market.

Thus, we come to perhaps the most important characteristic of a free market: the ability to live with uncertainty. For a free market to self-organize and search for a solution, the participants must not try to impose solutions on the group as a whole. If state controls *impede* the search process, then a solution may never be found. Thus, when a governing body must do something, Hayek says that it must take a "form [that] will least interfere with the functioning of the market" and "preserve competition." The emerging markets in Asia and eastern Europe are now facing the most dire economic crisis since World War II. With no tradition of free-market economics, these countries may not be prepared for the uncertainty that arises with crisis. They may not realize that living with that uncertainty is part of having a free-market economy. If the people demand state controls, economic matters, in the long run, will only stagnate.

SUMMARY

In this chapter, we looked at the nature of the creative process. We saw that the entrepreneurial spirit had much in common with the creative process of individuals. In both cases, living with uncertainty was a necessary element for the creative act. Creative achievers are often those who can live with the uncertainty of the creative process and persist while a solution is sought. A free market needs to do the same. If the free market cannot live with uncertainty, then it will become like a noncreative individual, unable to adapt, grow, and innovate, and stagnation will follow. Uncertainty is the price of innovation and adaptation.

Given that uncertainty is necessary for innovation and adaptability, what are the limits to structure? Many Asian countries have strong central governments. Can such a system be consistent with the uncertainty that is necessary if the benefits of free markets are to be felt? In the next chapter, we will examine this question: Can structure and free markets coexist?

CHAPTER 10

Rules and Law:
Limits in Complexity

*But rightful liberty is unobstructed action according to our will
within limits drawn around us by the equal rights of others.*
　　　　　　　　　　　　　　　　　—Thomas Jefferson

*The avowed aim of all utopian movements is to put an end to
history and to establish a final and permanent calm.*
　　　　　　　　　　　　　　　　　—Ludwig von Mises

W E have dealt with decentralization, feedback, innovation,
and adaptation in complex systems. We have also seen
how these relate to the Austrian school of economics. The final
element of complexity, as defined in Chapter 4, is *rules*. Rules
are not discussed much in the complexity literature because
complexity is interested in natural systems. In these systems,
rules take the form of physical laws so they are taken for
granted. In social systems such as economics or the arts, rules
usually evolve to become laws, often imposed by governing
bodies. Because of this distinction, there has long been a feeling in academia that social systems are inherently different

from physical systems. That may or may not be true. Certain social systems, such as the ironically named "socialism," have little in common with physical laws. However, as we shall see, a hallmark of a free society is its ability to evolve over time. The optimal environment for doing so has much in common with physical systems. In this chapter, we will look first at the nature of physical law, then at the nature of social laws. By contrasting the two, we can make conjectures as to the type of social system that would be the most adaptable. We can distinguish between these *adaptable* systems and other types of social systems in current use. We will find that, in social systems, there is a trade-off between free and structured societies. Structured societies have greater short-term stability and less uncertainty; however, they are less adaptable and offer less opportunity to their citizens. Structured societies are less stable over the long term. A free society, on the other hand, is less stable in the short term but more stable in the long term. In particular, a free society is more creative and adaptable. Its citizens are offered more opportunity. The price for this opportunity is uncertainty for the individual even as there is greater stability for the whole. At times, the price of freedom is high. A key danger is that the citizens will give up on the system during bad times because the uncertainty is simply too much to live with.

This discussion will, of necessity, be somewhat simplistic. However, the ideas here should be useful in determining which kind of laws best suit a free society.

PHYSICAL LAWS

Basic laws are often referred to as "first principles." Euclid called them *axioms*. They are the beginning of everything—statements accepted without proof. Newton based his physics on some of basic laws of motion, such as force equals mass times acceleration $(F = M \cdot A)$. Einstein deduced his famous mass/energy conservation law: energy equals mass times the speed of light squared $(E = MC^2)$. This law came from Einstein's insight that the speed of light was a constant—another law. Physical laws usually deal with limits. They express how far things can go. According to Einstein's formula, we cannot travel faster than the speed of light because, as we approach the speed of light, our mass becomes infinite. In physics and chemistry, physical laws state the limits of nature.

We can use physical laws to our advantage. For instance, there are laws that govern the behavior of gases and liquids. Normally, water cannot be heated above 100 degrees Centigrade because it turns into steam (a gas) at that point. However, the laws regarding pressure, volume, and temperature allow us to "superheat" water at temperatures higher than boiling, without evaporation, by keeping the water under high pressure. We can then use superheated water in heating systems, for instance.

Axioms in mathematics are slightly different. Mathematics is, after all, a human creation. Unlike physical laws, which are set by nature, mathematical axioms are created by mathematicians. They are still "first principles" such as the Commutative Law: If $a = b$, then $b = a$. They are statements made without proof. For a mathematical system to qualify as a true system, it must be proven to obey basic laws such as the Commutative Law, the Associative Law, and the Distributive Law. One widely used system involves "complex numbers." The square root of -1 exists in complex numbers, whereas it does not exist in the set of real numbers. In mathematics, new laws are often "discovered" but not in the sense of physical systems, though there may be a relationship with the real world. Even so, mathematical laws, like physical laws, are limits. If mathematical laws were allowed to be broken, the whole system would collapse. If physical laws were changed, the fabric of our universe would change.

That does not mean that our *conception* of physical law cannot change. We often find that "laws" discovered earlier are not really general cases. Newton's laws of motion, for instance, work most of the time. However, as the speed of light is approached, they break down. Einstein adapted Newton's laws for discoveries that were outside of Newton's knowledge base. We often find that earlier laws were actually "wrong" in the sense that, like Newton's laws, they applied only within a limited framework.

In complex systems, physical laws also become constraints, or rules. The threads-to-buttons rule, for instance, determines the minimum level of connections needed for complexity to exist. The level of feedback in a system can also be determined by these rules. Per Bak, at the Santa Fe Institute, has long worked with one of the simplest complexity models built around sand piles. It begins with a metal plate. Sand is dropped onto the plate one grain at a time. A pile of sand develops as the plate fills, and a conical heap begins to grow. After a time, the slope of the sides of the sand pile stops growing. The sand pile has reached a critical state. At this point, adding a grain of sand makes the pile less stable. As new grains are dropped, sand slides begin to develop. Some are small, some are large. However, the slope of the sides of the pile remains constant. The size of the slides varies and is completely unpredictable. The slope is also completely predictable. Once again, we have global structure and local uncertainty. The slope of the sand pile is a natural law. It is the global structure of this complex system. It is also a limit. The slope cannot grow beyond that point and still be a complex structure.

In other complex structures, we find the same characteristic. The global structure follows some form of natural law. Remember the oak tree? Each oak tree has the same *type* of leaves and the same *type* of bark. However, each individual oak tree has a different shape, a different number of leaves, and a different number of branches. The details that differentiate each oak tree are determined by random factors such as the weather and the type of soil the seed fell in. The global characteristics that unite oak trees as a species, however, are determined by natural law, embedded in the genetic code of an oak's DNA.

When a complex process self-organizes, it does so under conditions that are also determined by natural law. Take a fluid heated from below in a process called Raleigh–Bayard convection. At low levels of heat, the water becomes heated by convection and eventually reaches a uniform temperature. The water molecules all move independently. However, once the heat passes a critical threshold, the molecules begin behaving coherently. The water begins to follow a convection roll: the water heated below rises, then cools at the top and falls. The convection roll follows a circular path that can either be left or right. The direction of the roll cannot be predicted, but the fact that a roll will happen, once the temperature crosses the critical threshold, is known with certainty. To maintain the roll, the temperature must be kept at the critical level. Too high, and the water turns to steam, boiling chaotically. Too low, and there is no organization; there is merely a static, though stable structure. Natural law tells us that to maintain the convection roll, we must maintain the temperature at the critical level where self-organization occurs.

Even in this case, the physical law is a limitation. Temperature cannot fall outside of the critical level; if it does, the self-organizing behavior stops. In essence, we find that physical laws are limits on the process. If those limits are released, then the self-organizing structure either collapses to a static state or spins wildly out of control into chaos. A complex system sits on the edge of chaos, but has also passed beyond the static state. As we saw in Chapter 3, it sits balanced between the structure of the machine and the chaos of a free-flying balloon. This, of course, has implications for social systems as well. Predictability is largely tied to stability.

Stability and Predictability

In physical systems, we often look at a process in terms of its *predictability*, which is, after all, our prime measurement of uncertainty. A stable process is one that is predictable. Within the realm of predictability, we have long- and short-term abilities. Table 10.1 shows the four types of processes.

Type I: Simple Linear—High Long-Term and Short-Term Predictability

This type of process has a high degree of short-term and long-term predictability because there is a direct one-to-one correspondence between a factor and its impact on the process. For instance, we can observe that, for every point that interest rates

---

TABLE 10.1
Levels of Predictability

Short-Term Predictability		
High	Nonlinear Dynamic	Linear
Low	Nonlinear Stochastic	Complex
	Low	*High*
	Long-Term Predictability	

drop, stock prices rise by x percent. In a linear formula, there is no difference between the near term and the long term. A linear process is stable and has low uncertainty at both the long term and the short term, as long as the system remains closed. These are the simplest processes to study. Unfortunately, in real life, very few systems are actually driven by linear relationships. The ones that exist, however, cannot stand up to exogenous shocks. A clockworks is a linear system. It runs fine until something gums it up.

Type II: Nonlinear Dynamic (Chaos)—High Short-Term Predictability; Low Long-Term Predictability

A chaotic process is one in which the relationship between the factors and the process is exponential. It is like the old story of the straw that breaks the camel's back. Load up a camel with goods and the camel is still standing. Continue to load on more goods, and, eventually, there will be so much weight that any additional weight, even a straw, will make the camel fall down. It is not the weight of the straw itself that the camel cannot hold. It is the cumulative weight. This is a nonlinear reaction. When a many-factored process like the weather is considered, a small effect can cause a large reaction later on. These "chaotic" processes can often be predicted over the short term because the near-term relationship is almost linear. Look at the shape of the earth in your own neighborhood, and the earth looks flat. Only by traveling a far distance into space can the roundness be perceived. So it is with a nonlinear relationship. In the near term, it is almost linear; but the farther you move away from your current position, the more nonlinear it becomes. Thus, a nonlinear dynamic system (often referred to as a "chaotic" system) is predictable in the short term, but unpredictable in the long term.

A chaotic system has great short-term stability, but its long-term stability is unknown. An exogenous shock to a chaotic system sends it into an entirely different path.

Type III: Nonlinear Stochastic (Probabilistic Chaos)— Low Short-Term and Long-Term Predictability

Another type of nonlinear relationship is a nonlinear stochastic one. It is wrongly assumed that the normal distribution (or bell-shaped curve) defines most types of "disorderly" processes. Unfortunately, there are many that do not fill this criterion, and the probabilities for them are quite different. Although difficult to specify, a nonlinear stochastic process is one in which the probabilities change regularly. They never converge to a set distribution such as the bell-shaped curve.

Type IV: Complex—High Long-Term Predictability; Low Short-Term Predictability

Complex processes, as we have said, are characterized by global structure and local randomness. These characteristics can be translated into high long-term and low short-term predictability. The global structure allows us to predict the typical characteristics, but not the details. For an oak tree, we can predict the *type* of leaves and bark, but not the number of leaves or branches. For Raleigh–Bayard convection, we can predict when the convection rolls will begin, but not their direction. In a complex process, such as a simple game of poker, we could predict our cumulative winnings from playing thousands of hands, but not our take or our loss from any one hand. Complexity allows us to predict results after the long term, but the near term is unknown and unknowable. If it were predictable, as in simple poker, then the process would no longer be complex, and we would lose every hand.

Complex processes, as we have seen, are resilient to exogenous shocks. A complex process can learn from its shocks and still reach its goal through alternative paths. It is innovative, adaptable, and able to learn. It also self-organizes.

COMPLEX SOCIETY

Through our brief history, humanity has generally gone for stable and rigid social systems. Ancient civilizations such as the Egyptians, the Greeks, and the Romans all had fairly bureaucratic societies (even though the word *bureaucratic* was not coined until the nineteenth century). These were mostly closed societies, except in the business of trade.

In the twentieth century, we have had two broad types of societies: democratic and totalitarian. The democratic societies tend to be open or fluid, and they have free-market, capitalist economies. The capitalist economies have offered opportunity for great wealth, but there has always been disparity between the very wealthy and the very poor. The poor, having fewer resources than the rich, have not been able to maintain and exercise the rights they supposedly have in a free society. Thus, capitalism offered the opportunity for great wealth, but, by the late nineteenth century, seemed unable to deliver social justice. In addition, capitalism was prone to economic busts following the booms, so it seemed inefficient. Capitalism has had many advantages, but those advantages have tended to be concentrated in the hands of a few. Despite the promise of opportunity, the reality of wealth disparity and inefficiency has caused many to search for alternative models.

As we discussed earlier, the socialist style of government became a threat to free societies in the mid-twentieth century. For some time, socialism had been considered an alternative to capitalism because they offered both efficiency and social justice. Many intellectuals were socialists. In 1928, the playwright, George Bernard Shaw published *The Intelligent Woman's Guide to Socialism and Capitalism*. In the foreword, he states that he is writing this guide (which extols the virtues of socialism) for women so he can "get at American men through American women."

Socialism was supposed to be a system in which the state owned the industries, and the state, in turn, was owned by the workers. So, the workers had indirect ownership of industry through the state. In the nineteenth century, when workers had no rights, this seemed like a fair alternative. The economy itself would be run by a central organizing committee, to ensure that the bottlenecks and shortages that caused economic collapses in capitalist societies would not happen. Thus, socialism, in its original conception, would offer social justice within a "classless" society, and economic efficiency through central planning. The Russians, under V.I. Lenin, set up a socialist state in which the workers were ruled by the Communist Party. The workers, in theory, owned the state, but the state was actually run by a committee and, eventually, by a dictator—the Party Secretary. All industries were nationalized. Each industry was run by the state in a strictly organized manner, and each industry leader received instructions from the state, which coordinated all resources and production. The government and the economy were run according to very strict rules. Little or no flexibility was allowed. Individual initiative was discouraged; the individual was to be absorbed into the faceless masses. The individual's own life was meaningless. Only the state mattered. The state would offer the people efficiency and social justice through a classless society.

What went wrong? It took many years, but *everything* went wrong. The idea of a classless society went by the boards very quickly. In theory, the workers ran the state, which controlled production. In reality, a new ruling class was created through the Communist Party. The centralization of power resulted in not only a single political party dictatorship (which suppressed opposing views) but eventually a single-person dictatorship, with Joseph Stalin assuming all power. In the end, communism was no different from any other totalitarian government in countries such as Nazi Germany or Fascist Italy, where the state controlled the industries. In addition, state control of industry turned out to be inefficient at levels rarely experienced by a major world power. The capitalist West had already discovered that bureaucracy creates inefficiency because it focuses workers on internal matters rather than on helping their customers. The Soviets created the same bureaucratic mentality at the state level. By retaining power, the government existed to serve itself rather than the people. Workers were not encouraged to display initiative because that ruffled the feathers of those in charge of the bureaucracy. Shortages in consumer goods developed regularly. The standard of living of the people as a whole was far below that of other industrialized nations. The business cycle, instead of being smoothed to a high level of productivity, was stuck at a low level. Whatever goods were produced were of low quality because the producers had no incentive (through competition) to improve them. If a company is the only one making cars, why try to make them better? The system eventually collapsed in a mass of inefficiency. The recent Russian experiment with free markets also seems to have failed. We will discuss the reasons below.

Communism still lives in China and Cuba. Socialist doctrine continues to be discussed. With the collapse of the Russian capitalist experiment, there is a danger that that part of the world will slide back into socialism. What does socialism promise that is so appealing? Certainty. Ironically, a far "left" government offers a life without change, which the West considers a "conservative" attribute. At this point, it is helpful to contrast the various types of economic and social models.

SOCIAL LAW

Social laws, at their core, deal with rights. These can be the rights of individuals or of the state. The emphasis on rights shows the kind of government we are dealing with. Either way, the rest of the laws, like physical laws, deal with limits—what citizens are not allowed to do because it violates the rights of either other individuals or the state.

In democratic societies, the rights of individuals are "first principles." Thus, the first ten amendments to the U.S. Constitution are called the "Bill of Rights" because they explicitly lay out the rights of individuals alongside the structure of government. All other laws must conform to the Bill of Rights. Individuals cannot violate the rights of other individuals. Such activities are illegal. Capital crimes, such as murder, are illegal. Individuals also have property rights. The right to own and sell personal property is also an important component of the democratic legal system. Some things, however, cannot be owned if ownership would be to the detriment of others. Sources of water, for instance, are considered the property of the general public and are administered by the state. Property ownership extends to intellectual property, an example of the adaptive nature of the law. Limits are set on how individuals can affect other individuals, and the state cannot do anything that affects the rights of individuals except in an emergency, such as during a war. Abraham Lincoln, the Great Emancipator, suspended individual rights during the Civil War as a matter of national security. Otherwise, the laws set limits on individual actions. Unless explicitly prohibited by law, individuals are free to follow their pursuits.

These rules have evolved through a manner of natural selection that is not unlike Darwinian evolution or genetic algorithms. Hayek (1973) said, "Rules will always operate in competition and combination with other rules" and "whether a rule will prevail in a particular case will depend on the strength of the propensity it describes." In other words, rules compete with one another. The strongest survive. Rules are often combined, and the offspring may replace the parents. The strongest rules are accepted by the general population and become laws. Laws are rules that are adopted by the legislative bodies as final. Hayek said that man is "governed by rules which have by a process of selection evolved in the society in which he lives." The order that emerges from the adaptation of these rules is critical in understanding a free market. In Chapter 3, we spoke of the *typical* and *unique* features of a complex system. The rules adopted by a complex society affect its typical features; that is, the rules governing human behavior, not the actions of specific individuals, are those adopted. Interestingly, *cultural* rules fall under the latter category. Each culture has its own taboos. In most (but not all) Western cultures, polygamy is outlawed. Rules like this are unique to each culture. On the other hand, murder is almost universally condemned, particularly if it is done for personal rather than political reasons. The rules that are universally adopted affect the global structure, leaving the unique details to develop over time.

In communist systems, the rights of the people as a whole are more important than individual rights. Thus, the state, representing "the people" as a collective, has rights that supersede the rights of individuals. In the Soviet system, for instance, there was no ownership of personal property. Everything belonged to the state. Laws largely examined the rights of the state vs. the rights of individuals. Limits were set on what individuals could do, rather than stating what they could not do. This system appeals to individuals who find freedom a burden and will join mass movements to escape individual responsibility. Earlier, we discussed how our imagination can create patterns from the vague shapes we see in a dark room. These patterns help us to impose order on the unknown, even if the order is an illusion. Likewise, the promise of order within a totalitarian society can become more important than individual freedom if the latter causes anxiety. A Nazi Youth goal in the 1930s was: "To be free from freedom." Socialist totalitarianism offered the same comfort, but the citizens living under its rules paid a great price.

Physical law resembles democratic law, in theory. Physical laws draw boundaries around what nature can do. As long as it does not break physical law, then nature is free to do what it likes. Physical law, like democratic law, tells the process what it cannot do rather than what it can. Nature is free to evolve within this structure. Communist law, on the other hand, gives instructions to its citizens. Communist laws are not really rules governing proper behavior, they are commands of what an individual should and should not do. Life under communism has traffic lights. Either stop or go; there is no in-between or other alternative. As a result, there is no room for improvisation and creativity. When told what to do, you cannot innovate without breaking the law. The communist process essentially became frozen at an early stage. Democracy has some laws that are commands (traffic laws, for instance), but the main purpose of the body of laws is to create rules of conduct, not commands.

FREE VS. STRUCTURED MARKETS

Economic theory is commonly separated from political theory, but it is difficult to do so because the kind of economic environment that exists depends largely on the rights of individuals. A free market requires an environment that is focused on individual rights. A structured economy expects each individual to follow the dictates of the state for the good of the whole. In this discussion, we will focus mostly on Western democracy and communist socialism (monarchy, for instance, will not be discussed). Democracy and capitalism tend to go together because both are concerned with the rights or opportunities of the individual. Socialism is concerned with the needs of the state—meaning the people as a whole—and less concerned with individual rights or opportunities. However, there are shades of gray within both systems, and many countries have a hybrid of the two. China, for instance, is still a communist state, but it is instituting some free-market elements. Many European governments have capitalist-style markets, but they offer citizens a mandatory amount of state-run services. The United States has very free markets and offers little in the way of "safety nets" for individuals, compared to European states. Is there a correct balance? Like many of the questions we have raised in this book, there is no "right" answer. The outcome depends on the goals of the people and the amount of uncertainty that they are willing to live with. Uncertainty is the price we pay for freedom. Many people are willing to give up their freedom for a more certain environment, but, in doing so, they pay a price in lost opportunity.

Most governments are concerned with two things: (1) the rights of the people, and (2) the economic well-being of the people. "The people" can mean individuals or the state as a collective of individuals. Even in totalitarian states such as Nazi Germany, these concerns exist. They were considered dependent on the well-being of Adolph Hitler, but they were still a part of National Socialism. Free societies and socialist societies have their own advantages and disadvantages.

Free Societies

Advantages

In theory, a free society offers a high level of *opportunity* to all of its citizens. Anyone with a good idea can, through persistence and risk taking, rise up through the levels of business. Bill Gates rose from a modest background and became the richest man in the world in only ten years. The credo of capitalist democracies is that people who work hard can achieve much in the way of material gain. Those who are born into wealth have an advantage, but anyone can rise up through the ranks. Individuals are free to pursue whatever dream they have, as long as it's legal and they can support themselves. The result is a population that is constantly in touch with most other parts of society, establishing links through knowledge sharing and free communication among the participants. This communication, in turn, encourages the stabilizing force of cooperation. Hayek (1948) said, "What a free society offers to the individual is much more than what he would be able to do if only he were free." The collective society benefits from allowing individual freedom.

Because of the opportunity provided, there is *a fluid social structure*. In the United States, many of the people we most admire—say, Abraham Lincoln or John D. Rockefeller—came from poor backgrounds and achieved prominent positions. Being born into a working-class background does not limit people to staying in the working class, unless they want to. And, someone from a wealthy background can still become a carpenter if that work is found to be rewarding.

Because opportunity and social mobility are available, there is *a high level of innovation* in the economy and in society. Individual initiative by entrepreneurs is highly prized. Anyone with a good idea and the ability to *sell* the idea can probably gain the financing needed to develop the idea. The level of innovation is also associated with luck. Many lucky opportunities present themselves to people, though only a special kind of person may recognize an opportunity when it presents itself. An unknown person noticed that a special kind of clay was being used to soak up oil spills in garages. He thought that perhaps the same material could have other uses as well. The industry dedicated to hygiene for cats was born from this insight. Communication links, including word-of-mouth, allow entrepreneurs to be on a constant lookout for new consumer needs.

Finally, free societies have *a high level of adaptability.* Innovation is the way to get ahead in a capitalist society. As a result, a large portion of the population is devoted to innovation. This also allows for adaptability. Because innovators constantly seek new applications of existing technology, problem solving is already a part of the culture. When crises arise, problem solving is already going on. During crises, it is directed toward a "presented" problem rather than a "found" problem.

Disadvantages

Wealth is unevenly distributed in a capitalist system. Many people inherit their wealth. Individuals have the right to pass the fruit of their labor to their descendants—after the amount prescribed by inheritance tax laws is collected by the state for redistribution to the less advantaged. Many other people accumulate wealth through their own labor. Frugality, family circumstances, hard work, or luck can affect the final amount. Still, there are always the very poor and the very rich. Equal opportunity does not mean equal wealth. As a result, *political power is also unevenly distributed.* In *The Theory of Choice,* Robert Sugden says, "If we want the standard of living that only the market can provide, we must accept that social justice is unattainable." The wealthy have the power to keep themselves wealthy and others poor.

Closely connected to uneven distribution is the fact that there are always *winners and losers.* Equal talent or opportunity does not guarantee success. There are, in fact, no guarantees. Some people who have higher skills simply do not get the breaks. Good luck sometimes follows those with less technical skills but more social skills. Thus, less talented people may attain positions of authority because of their social skills rather than their ability to get a job done. The historian Will Durant said, "For freedom and equality are sworn and everlasting enemies, and when one prevails the other dies." Durant was not referring to equal opportunity, but to a classless society in which everyone is supposed to share wealth and power.

Less control over society is another factor. The very mobility that gives a free society its greatest attribute also makes it easier for criminals to take unfair advantage. Controls are always being put in place, but they are constrained by the very liberties of those whom the law is trying to protect. Sometimes, so that all individuals can be protected, criminals are released unpunished. In the United States, an individual must be read his or her rights when being arrested. This law is specifically designed so that innocent people know how to achieve their release. However, if these rights are not read, guilty people will also be released. The rights of all individuals are more important than the punishment of one individual for a specific crime.

Finally, *a free society is always in a high state of uncertainty.* There are no guarantees in a free society. Even someone who has attained or was born to great wealth and power may be penniless or in jail in a very brief time. People take risks to make "the big score." Sometimes it pays off, but most of the time it does not. In a capitalist society, even working hard and staying loyal may not pay off, as many employees discovered when the downsizing during the early 1990s eliminated their jobs. The cost of opportunity is the risk of loss. It could happen at any time, to anyone. In capitalist societies, there are various sayings that cover these events. "What goes up must come down" refers to the stock market, and "The party's over" refers to the end of good times.

The Future

In free markets, the long term cannot be predicted in detail. It is described only broadly, in the form of goals. Plans can be made for the near term to a fair degree, but plans beyond a year are considered outlines. Capitalist societies know that the further ahead something is planned, the less likely the plans will come to fruition because so many paths criss-cross on the way to achieving goals. Most successful people have only vague long-term plans, though they have goals that earn their persistence. What is not rigid is the way they achieve their goals. Like creative people, successful people are fluid about their near-term goals, but their long-term goal does not vary. We must all plan within short-term uncertainty to achieve long-term goals.

This uncertainty is not the same as risk. It is true uncertainty; that is, as individuals in a free society, we must face the fact that there are no real ways to assess the probabilities of our decisions. We are faced with numerous opportunities. Any action can have unintended consequences. However, uncertainty is also the source of opportunity. There may not be a "loss" involved, so the uncertainty is not "risk" in the probability sense. It can be useful or not, but it is not necessarily bad.

In theory, free societies are Type IV processes, as described earlier. They are characterized by a complexity created by local uncertainty and global stability. Although they are adaptable and innovative, they are subject to cycles of high and low productivity, in addition to diversity in the fates of the individual participants. Free societies keep their eyes to the future. They aim for progress, and they thrive on short-term change to achieve their long-term goals. They also self-organize, which is why those of us who live in a free society often see conspiracies where there are none. We see the vestiges of the loose links that connect us. We know that there are more of them than there should be in a random process. Because we know that the enemy is usually organized, we postulate that a Moriarty is behind it all. But the only organization is our own.

Free societies balance cooperation and competition. Cooperation keeps the global structure stable, and competition encourages change.

Socialism

Advantages

In theory, a socialist system should have *an even distribution of wealth*. Because everyone owns a share of all production, all workers should share evenly in the advantages. Like "equal opportunity" in capitalist systems, this is largely a dream of the process, though capitalist systems are a little closer to their ideal than socialist systems have been.

There should be a *classless social system.* If everyone has equal wealth, there is no stratification in society. Power, likewise, is equal among all. Fidel Castro tried a moneyless society in Cuba for a brief period. The idea was that, without money, there would be no class structure; everyone would have equal access to all goods. Unfortunately, the idea did not work. Without the incentive of earnings, production fell. The peso was reinstated. In the Soviet system, political power continued to be held by a few, who also kept a larger share of the wealth for themselves.

In a socialist system, there would be *no business cycle.* The booms and busts of capitalist systems would be replaced by a cycleless time of even production. The economy would always be in equilibrium. Unfortunately, this ended up being a low-level equilibrium.

Finally, *people would know their place.* As a structured society, there would be low uncertainty. Everyone could expect to be cared for by the state, which would make all decisions. Individuals would not have to worry about their future. The state would take care of all their needs. In theory, there would be no greed, no crime, and no hunger.

Disadvantages

In socialism, there are *no individual rights.* There is little opportunity for individuals to choose a profession or a lifestyle that suits their own goals. There can be no individual goals. Life is devoted to the collective, which is represented by the state. Growth of the individual, being unnecessary, is discouraged.

Decisions are made by a select few. The collective is represented by the workers' party, and all decisions are made by the party leaders. There is little opportunity for new ideas to take hold because the party is made up of those who have been around the longest. This group is closed. There is little incentive for them to admit new members who may have different views. The workers have no way to express their own ideas.

Because there is no opportunity for individual initiative, there is *a low level of innovation.* Thinking contrary to the collective is discouraged because it would reassert the rights of the individual. As a result, there is no search process for new ways of performing existing processes.

Finally, because there is a low level of innovation, there is also *low adaptability.* During a crisis, innovative thinking is usually required because the crisis is something that has never happened before. A committee, even in a western society, is slow to come to a group consensus. Innovative thinking has been discouraged all along, so new ideas are alien to the culture. The rigidity of the social fabric does not allow for solutions to a crisis.

The Future

In a socialist society, as in a utopian philosophy, the future is known with a high degree of certainty. The long term is merely the sum of all the near-term moments. Everything is planned. Everything is organized. There is no contingency that is not anticipated and dealt with. Utopian societies want no further change, just a prolonged "calm." Their goal is not progress, but keeping the status quo.

You probably know people who run their lives like socialists. They have their lives planned out: whom they will marry, when they will marry, how many children they will have, when they will become a corporate vice president, when they will take over as president, what colleges their children will attend, when they will retire. Such people are almost always disappointed. Something always interferes with their plans. These people think in a linear fashion. They are not resilient to changes in their environment. Neither were the communists.

In theory, socialist and other utopian societies are Type I systems. They have both long-term and short-term predictability. However, they are not resilient to shocks. They have to remain fully closed systems because any outside shocks will cause them to collapse. Hence, the Soviet Union kept its society closed; access by outsiders was limited. The Soviets expanded their realm by expanding their borders. Any nation brought into their sphere of influence was also cut off from outside influences. Social societies can only be consciously organized. They cannot organize themselves. Thus, when crisis strikes, members of socialist societies wait for orders. They take no initiative. Socialism is all cooperation and no competition. There is no incentive for change.

Anarchy

Societies living under conditions of continuous anarchy, such as Bosnia or Lebanon, have high uncertainty at both the long-term and short-term horizons. Moment to moment, life is unpredictable. The future is completely unknown. Such conditions generate extreme adaptability, but each innovation passes quickly from memory. Conditions never improve. There is no progress. Anarchic states are Type III societies characterized by stochastic chaos. Things change rapidly but never settle down to either a local or a global structure. There is not only no present, but no future either. Anarchic societies do not organize, either consciously or spontaneously; there is no time. When organization is finally suggested, the world has moved on. Anarchy, in fact, is unrestrained competition without the stabilizing effects of cooperation. Everyone is acting in his or her own self-interest; there is no thought of others. Without cooperation, there are no links and no spontaneous organization, only chaos.

Free Markets and the Need for Uncertainty

Free markets need rules and structure, but they also need uncertainty. What kind of rules do not constrain uncertainty? First, we need rules that prevent people from infringing on the rights of others. Anything that would allow one individual to interfere with the rights of another is forbidden. The rules that guarantee individual rights also encourage cooperation and trust. A policy of equal rights under the law ensures awareness that no person can legally take advantage of another. This, in turn, encourages the cooperation that is necessary for stability. This sequence does not *always* work, but it achieves a great degree of success. Second, we need property rights to ensure that individuals can retain the fruits of their own labor. Finally, we need rules to ensure competition. For free markets, this is crucial. Unfortunately, the Austrians, particularly Hayek, came to the conclusion that because the consequences of government regulation could not be predicted, there should be no regulation. The free market should decide. Hayek and the Austrians are operating under a number of mistaken assumptions.

A key error is that they assume that the free market makes optimal decisions. We have already seen that evolutionary paradigms, including that of the Austrians, do not necessarily make optimal decisions. They also assumed that the outcome of an unregulated society is free competition. Unfortunately, history has shown otherwise. Until Teddy Roosevelt became president, the outcome of laissez-faire economics was monopoly, not competition. Thus, our regulatory laws are firmly tied to ensuring competition. This is a reflection of natural law, which tries to keep competition going. If the foxes eat all the rabbits, the foxes will eventually starve. Because the rabbits have a competitive advantage in their fast breeding, the foxes and at least some rabbits survive. So it is with the law in free markets. Without regulation, competition would eventually die, as would the free market. Regulation, rather than making the environment more structured, actually ensures that no one has a monopoly, and it keeps uncertainty high by keeping the environment competitive.

So it is with social law. In a free society, equal opportunity keeps competition alive among the participants, thus ensuring that uncertainty remains high. No one in a free society can rest on his or her laurels forever.

A free-market economy, and a free society, need uncertainty in order to maintain the innovation and adaptability that are synonymous with a free-market economy. Structured societies such as socialism and other utopian constructs try to do away with uncertainty through planning. Although they seemingly eliminate short-term uncertainty, they do so at a price. Eliminating uncertainty through the rigorous use of rules also eliminates the ability to innovate and adapt. As a result, if there are changes to the environment of a structured society, it will eventually become extinct because it is unable to evolve to a new state that can handle the changed circumstances. Thus, free markets need uncertainty in order to remain free.

In modern society, there are degrees of social order. Many new states are trying free-market systems and are finding the price too high. Still others, like China, are trying hybrid approaches. Are such approaches valid? If so, how much can be expected of them? In the next chapter, we will examine these questions.

CHAPTER 11

Degrees of Order: Balancing Rules, Freedom, and Uncertainty

> *. . . by rules rather than by specific commands it is possible to make use of knowledge which nobody possesses as a whole.*
> —Friedrich A. Hayek

ALTHOUGH the world has turned more and more toward free-market systems since the collapse of communism, there are many different forms of capitalism just as there are many different forms of democracy. The American style of government and economic structure has not been duplicated elsewhere. Most free-market countries, even those of Europe, are more structured and more centralized than the U.S. model.

The American form of democracy, which separates the executive, legislative, and judicial branches, thus decentralizing power, is rarely used. Instead, the older British form of parliamentary government, with combined executive and legislative branches, is much more common. Likewise, the U.S. economic model, which has less regulation or government participation in

185

business, remains different from those in most other regions of the world. Government participation in business and in provision of a minimal standard of living is more widely adapted in the rest of the industrialized world. The U.S. Government guarantees less to its citizens than do governments in other countries. Americans live with more uncertainty than do people in any other major nation that is not at war.

Yet, the United States is the world's dominant power, particularly from an economic standpoint. Why? There are many conflicting opinions. In this chapter, we will look at the relationship between structure and freedom. We will try to find the mix that is "optimal" enough to promote the future welfare of both the individual and the collective.

STRUCTURE AND LAW

The more structured the environment, as we discussed in Chapter 10, the less individual freedom there is. As we said, in a free society, the law sets limits on what people can do. However, the purpose of law is to restrain people so they do not "commit aggression on the equal rights of others," to quote Thomas Jefferson. Cicero said, "The more laws, the less justice." A more modern credo would be: *The more laws, the less freedom.*

In a structured society, the laws tell people what they can do. Everything else is forbidden. This approach is very different from the intent of democratic laws. It is a *command* approach; it assumes that those in command know what is best for everyone. Cooperation is enforced.

In reality, most nations have some combination of structure and freedom. If we accept that spontaneous organization in economic life offers the most opportunity but also the most potential for poverty, what combination of structure and freedom would be optimal? Is the Chinese approach of loosening some economic freedoms while tightening others going to work? Is the laissez-faire approach advocated by the Austrian school really practical?

We will examine potential answers to these questions.

THE COMPLEXITY MODEL

In this section, I propose a model that incorporates the trade-off among uncertainty, structure, and innovation.

Structure and Uncertainty

A complex process is balanced between a static linear process and a nonlinear chaotic one. The three states—static, complex, and chaotic—represent potential environments for economic systems. Utopian societies, including the socialist model, favor the static state. This includes all "command" governments that tell citizens what they *can* do. Everything else is illegal. Chaos would reign in all states ruled by anarchy. War-torn Bosnia, or Lebanon in the 1980s and early 1990s, belongs to this category. Free societies fall under the umbrella of complex systems, where day-to-day freedom gives way to self-organizing behavior and long-term stability. No government is pure in any of the three states. All lie along a continuum of uncertainty/structure. Those with low uncertainty have high structure.

Figure 11.1 graphs a line that represents my subjective opinion of various world governments. At the level of low uncertainty and high structure lies communist Cuba. Iraq, Iran, and Libya could also be included. All are totalitarian states. Individual freedoms are not allowed because of either ideology or religion. These countries are followed by China. The Chinese

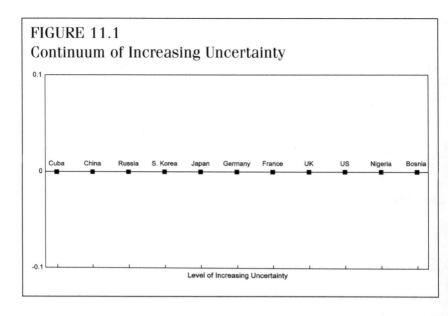

FIGURE 11.1
Continuum of Increasing Uncertainty

government has initiated some free-market reforms while keeping a firm hold on its power. The Russian government has tried free-market reforms, but still has control of many industries. Next come the Asian markets, represented here by South Korea and Japan. Japan has democratic elections and a free-market system, but the government sets industrial policy, and Japanese corporations, following long tradition, acquiesce. In the post-World War II era, the Ministry of Finance specified that Japan should pursue heavy industries, so the Japanese built foundries and made high-quality steel cheaply. In the 1950s, manufacturing was the future of Japan, and the automobile industry was born. In the 1960s and 1970s, the future was electronics. In each case, new initiatives were dictated by the government, and industry followed suit. Although successful, this is still more structure than most industrialized nations have, and places "Japan, Inc." not far from Russia. Japan, as has been argued for some time, is not a very competitive environment. Outside competition is restricted to the protection of domestic providers.

Next come the industrialized nations of Europe, followed by the United States. European governments, although they divested themselves of state industries during the 1980s, still have a stronger hand in business than does the U.S. Government. They have more social programs and more generous state-run retirement programs. Restrictions on foreign governments are common, and they in turn restrict competition. The U.S. Government regulates certain industries (like the cable TV industry), but it has continued to expand deregulation. Even electric utilities are losing their state-run monopolies and have begun competing.

At the end of the spectrum are countries in anarchy: Nigeria and Bosnia. Here there are no rules, but no competition either.

This list is limited, but think of other countries you know or read about. Where would they fit into this line? How much structure do they have? How much uncertainty do their citizens have to live with?

Innovation

The next dimension is the level of innovation in the system. However, there is not a linear, one-to-one correspondence between the ability to innovate and the level of structure. Instead, the relationship is nonlinear.

In natural systems, we have seen numerous examples of "phase transitions" or breakpoints where the nature of a process suddenly changes. When the ratio of threads to buttons crossed 0.50, the number of buttons in the largest cluster jumped from 12 percent to 85 percent. When the temperature of water passes the critical level, convection rolls begin. In each case, the transition from largely independent to self-organized behavior begins spontaneously when a certain critical level is crossed. In this model, I propose two breakpoints: (1) the jump from structured to complex behavior, and (2) the jump from complexity to chaos, or anarchy.

At low levels of freedom, there is little self-organization in market forces. Activity is largely dictated by the state. As controls are loosened and some market freedom is allowed, some entrepreneurial activity starts. However, the activity is like a fluid heated to a low temperature. The heat travels by convection alone, so there is only a slow process with no organization. Controls on individual freedoms are still high enough to restrict the diversity of knowledge among the participants. There is no "loose coupling" connecting the participants. The state still dictates many of the relationships. Individuals do not have a self-interest to act on. There is no self-organizing behavior. Innovative ability rises modestly, but is limited because the ruling body has limited knowledge.

As individual freedom rises, the level of connection and interdependence among the participants rises. Finally, the "heat" passes a critical level. Individuals, now able to act in their own self-interest, connect because of their shared knowledge base and their overlapping objectives. The economy self-organizes spontaneously, and true free markets are born. Innovative ability jumps up as the critical level is passed.

However, there comes a point where there are not enough rules to ensure that competition can continue. Either monopolies develop and the free market dies, or society itself breaks down and anarchy reigns. Individuals are only out for themselves. There is no structure, organized or self-organized. The level of innovation declines.

Figure 11.2 adds innovation to the time line of the previous chart. Again, the break points are subjective.

FIGURE 11.2
Uncertainty vs. Complexity

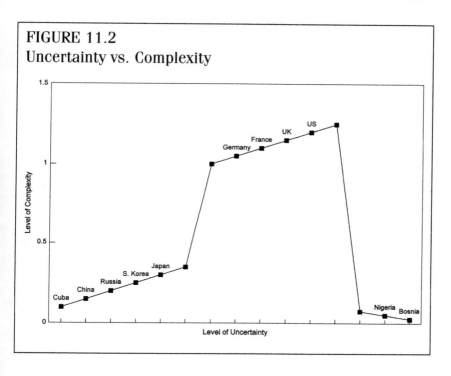

Cooperation and Competition

In the end, the three types of societies can be categorized according to the trade-off between cooperation and competition. In a utopian society, there is no competition. This is as true for the modern concept of socialism as it was for the original "Utopia" fantasized by Sir Thomas More. A utopian society is all cooperation. Everyone has an assigned role and performs it. The collective decides what that role should be. The individual is nothing but a part of the collective. Rules say what individuals can do. If the rules do not *say* you can do something, you cannot do it.

When a state of anarchy exists, there is nothing but competition. People are out for themselves. There are no rules. The byword is *Trust No One*, but there is no conspiracy, just chaos. There is no cooperation, no stability. The reality is: Adapt or die. The situation is ever changing, and only those who can quickly adapt will survive.

A free society tries to balance these two extremes. Laws limit the ability of the people to take advantage of one another, while offering the freedom to do most other things. This allows both cooperation and competition; that is, it allows the links between the participants that are necessary for cooperation, while keeping the competitive environment as open as possible. It creates stability and the ability to innovate, but, to exist, the participants must agree that no one can know exactly what is going on. The individuals are always in a state of uncertainty about the collective. That is the price of freedom.

IMPLICATIONS OF THE COMPLEXITY MODEL

Hybrid Capitalism

A number of countries are experimenting with free-market economics. They are trying to incorporate free-market elements while continuing to restrict individual freedoms and levels of uncertainty in society. China has loosened many economic restrictions, but continues to keep the "command" model for individual freedoms. Countries like Indonesia were run by "crony capitalism," where ties to those in political power determined economic power as well. Most of these countries believe that the gradual loosening of economic freedom will allow them to have the benefits of free-market economies without having to give up political power or grant individual freedom. The complexity model implies that only so much economic growth can be accomplished by these efforts. Although there can be some growth (especially in the beginning), those societies will never cross the "critical threshold" of individual freedom that is necessary to develop a true free-market, self-organizing economic structure. They will never achieve the balance of order and chance that is necessary for innovation to occur. Thus, those experiments are doomed to eventual failure. Crises will occur, but the structures are not in place for innovation and adaptation to occur. Instead, there will be the same nonadaptive response of straight socialism, followed by eventual collapse. This can only be avoided if less structure and more competitive uncertainty are allowed in their economies.

Other hybrid systems, like Japan's, are also doomed to stagnation because the freedom and openness necessary for true complexity do not exist. Japan is close; so is South Korea and some other Southeast Asian economies. They must go the extra mile. Japan, despite its wealth, has been stagnating for over eight years. The Japanese have kept their economy closed, and so have been unable to innovate. Japanese industry waits for the answers to come from the Ministry of Finance, which has done such an admirable job in the past. But the country is now in crisis. The Ministry committee, with its limited membership, does not have the knowledge that the free market as a whole has. The structured search for an answer continues to climb one hill in the fitness landscape at a time, before realizing that it's not the right hill. The true solution is out there, but checking one hill at a time takes a long time, and time is running out.

The Russian economy poses more serious problems. Free-market reforms and individual freedoms were slowly imposed as an experiment. However, there were few regulations to ensure either individual freedoms or market competition. Rules were put in place but not enforced. Far worse, the people were not prepared for the high level of uncertainty that comes with living in a free-market economy. They had seen the material wealth of the West, but no one told them the cost in individual uncertainty and lack of guarantees. The Russians, unlike the Poles, had no tradition of free markets. They were used to a structured environment in which the state took care of the citizens. They had a low standard of living, but it was guaranteed. In free-market economies, there are no guarantees. You can become wealthy, be poor, or just get by, but there are no guarantees. Individual initiative is rewarded. Status quo just scrapes by. The law, while not always popular (especially the tax law), must be obeyed for the good of all. Complexity needs uncertainty, as do free markets.

Government and Crisis

When a financial or economic crisis hits a free-market economy (as it inevitably will), there is a general feeling that "Someone should do something." The government should do something to help the people and punish those responsible for the current economic crisis. The Austrian response to potential government action is discouraging. The Austrian school, even in its present form, believes that the government should do nothing; that is, the free market, which consists of the collective knowledge of the participants, knows what is best. Hayek felt that government interference, at best, was powerless or, at worst, made conditions deteriorate further. The reason had to do with the definitions of uncertainty we face in real time. Hayek felt that the government can never know what the unintended consequences of its actions might be, so the best course was to do nothing. Let the free market decide. Conservative politics has embraced this attitude, and there are some reasonable examples. Surely, if the welfare program, which was originally designed as a safety net, becomes chronically abused, neither the public nor the individual benefits. On the other hand, contrary to popular myth, the majority of welfare recipients are not chronically on the rolls.

The idea that the poor should be left to themselves does not sit well with most people. This is particularly true if a large portion of the general public is suffering due to an economic downturn. After all, general economic disasters are no different than natural disasters such as floods and earthquakes. The victims did not bring their condition upon themselves. Besides, we have already seen examples where the free market does not make optimal decisions. In addition, that exemplary free-market institution, the stock market, is notorious for overreacting to both good and bad news. So, the Austrian contention that the free market's collective knowledge is genius does not hold water and gives little comfort in bad times.

The opposite reaction is to "protect the little guy" by taking the risk that brought so much unhappiness to everyone who was out of the market. In trying to lower "risk," uncertainty in the marketplace is also inadvertently reduced. We have seen in this book that there cannot be a free market without uncertainty, and uncertainty and risk are not necessarily the same thing. Imposing more structure on the market by specifying what people can do rather than what they cannot do, will stifle the creativity of the market and kill it. The cure would be worse than the disease. Adding structure would make a country slide left on the line of uncertainty and innovation represented in Figure 11.2. If too many rules are imposed, then a reverse-phase change can occur. Remember that a Raleigh–Bayard convection roll can only occur if the water temperature stays at the critical level. If it drops, the liquid cools and the spontaneous organization represented by the convection rolls also stops. Rules that restrict freedom could cut off the "heat" that keeps the free market going.

History is filled with examples of rules that were put in place *after* a crisis, to give the public a feeling that their leaders were "doing something." For instance, there are no corporations in the United Kingdom because of the South Sea Island bubble of the late eighteenth century. In that fiasco, speculators created bogus corporations, sold stock, and then absconded with the money. The corporations were set up to do things like "drain the Nile River." There was a craze to invest in these companies, much like the Internet stock craze of 1998, when companies with no earnings could sell for over $100 per share. When the bubble collapsed, the British government banned corporations. That is why British companies are limited partnerships and carry the familiar "Ltd." suffix instead of "Inc." as in the United States. Outlawing corporations was not the way to stop the problem of speculators robbing the public. *Disclosure* was the answer.

After an economic crisis, there is a tendency to punish the guilty. People then know that those who caused their suffering have been dealt with. As we discussed in Chapter 7, this only distracts from the fact that nothing is really being done to fix the situation.

What kind of rules are acceptable? Rules that promote competition. Thus, rules already in place to outlaw insider trading (that is, having information not available to the general public) are good rules. They keep the free market competitive. Rules against price fixing and collusion are another example. A rule that outlaws particular investment strategies because people can lose money at them is not OK; however, requiring full disclosure of the risks involved is. Outlawing a strategy like using futures contracts for leverage is contrary to the spirit of a free market; however, making any fund or money manager that uses leverage disclose that fact is perfectly acceptable.

Any rule that reduces uncertainty is usually a bad idea. Remember, uncertainty is not risk. Free markets need uncertainty.

Usually, a rule that reduces uncertainty also reduces competition. Active competition is the outward measure that uncertainty remains in play.

We also need rules that ensure cooperation. The simplest way to do this is to ensure the rights of individuals. In a free society, individuals are free to do anything that does not infringe on the rights of others. When these rights are upheld, individuals have the confidence and trust that encourage cooperative behavior, because they know they cannot legally be taken advantage of by others.

Finally, at a time of crisis, a temporary safety net is needed for those who are suffering. It is true that the whole may then suffer longer, but at least those at the bottom will not suffer as much. Even Hayek agreed that some degree of wealth distribution was needed to help those with genuine need. In an evolving free market economy, there are no guarantees beyond a minimal level, though rules that guarantee equal access to opportunity benefit the whole. Rules that make biases due to social circumstances illegal are perfectly acceptable. Offering help to those in need is also acceptable, as long as dependence does not develop as a result.

Rules that reduce true uncertainty and competition also reduce the complexity of the economy, making it more structured. Creating a police state to control crime destroys the very freedoms that the police are supposed to protect. Similarly, reducing competitive uncertainty destroys a free market.

The Asian Crisis of the Late 1990s

I am closing this chapter with a brief discussion of the emerging markets' economic crisis, which began in 1997 and continues as of this writing in late 1998. The Asian crisis happened because of poor banking practices that made credit easy, and rampant speculation with borrowed funds in the stock and real estate markets. The losses have been so horrific (up to 80 percent of the wealth in Southeast Asia may have been destroyed) that many in those markets are blaming free-market systems for their suffering. As a result, they are sliding back into more structured economies. Malaysia, which has restricted all conversions of funds into foreign currencies, was the first to blame its woes on currency speculators like George Soros. The fact that their currency was overvalued because of excessive borrowing in U.S. dollars is not mentioned. Russia has never had the ability to enforce regulations and collect taxes. As a result, the government is bankrupt and corruption is everywhere. Again, free markets are being blamed, and Russia is sliding back into a quasi-socialist structure. The Russian people know only that things were better under the USSR; there may have been chronic shortages, but at least the basics were available. Meanwhile, the phase of reforms that would give more freedom to individuals is put on hold. Russia will never experience a "phase change" to a true free market until individuals have more freedom, but it now looks like the Russian people will be waiting a long time. The Malaysians are sliding down the competitive uncertainty line and may have already "phase changed" to a less complex plane.

These countries are not going through anything that developed nations did not also go through at some point. Panics were once a regular part of the economic landscape, as were the depressions that soon followed. However, the West knew, in its historical memory, that these were normal events. We pay for the good times with bad times, but, over the long run, things improve. The reaction of these troubled countries will determine whether they will ever attain a true free market through that balance of order and chance that defines complexity.

THE FUTURE

Undoubtedly, at some future time, an economic crisis in the West will once again cause a loss of confidence. Currently, there is a high degree of optimism that severe downturns are a thing of the past. However, in 1926, Joseph Schumpeter wrote that the business cycle seemed to have become tamer because there had not been a severe economic downturn since 1873, some 53 years before. There was even optimism that the business cycle, through productivity gains, had finally reached an equilibrium level that would make panics a thing of the past. Schumpeter was skeptical, and so should we now be, about the prospects that the "Goldilocks economy" of the 1990s will last forever. If there were no uncertainty, then free markets, as we have seen all through this book, would die because there would be no competition, no creativity, and no innovation. The market would stagnate; it would become predictable and structured. It would, in fact, not be a free market at all. It would be utopia—a world without change. Time is change, as we defined it earlier, so it would be a world without time, which is impossible. Thus, we can only assume that the markets will continue to have contractions. We will continue to have bad times. We will continue to have uncertainty.

CHAPTER 12

The Need for Uncertainty

"You evidently don't know me," said he.
"On the contrary," I answered, "I think it is fairly evident I do."
—Holmes to Moriarty, "The Final Problem"

THE term *self-organization* sounds like an oxymoron. "Organization" implies planning and, of course, a planner behind it all. We have examined numerous examples of natural self-organization. Some of these, such as hurricanes and other weather patterns, have been familiar. In fact, when weather forecasters discuss potential hurricanes, they talk about storms becoming "organized" in the tropics. We have also seen smaller examples such as sand piles and Raleigh–Bayard convection.

It does not require a leap of imagination to see these self-organizing patterns in nature. However, the idea that human society could also be a self-organizing process is harder to accept. We often see allusions to society as an organism, but we have a more difficult time accepting that we may all be part of a larger structure of which we have only dim awareness. However, we often do have a feeling that something is going on around us, but we do not know what it is. Particularly when important events happen, like the assassination of President John F. Kennedy, it seems unbelievable that something of such far-reaching influence could have been the work of a lone and insignificant stock clerk. In examining such events closely, we see all kinds of relationships between seemingly unrelated parts of the story. This leads us to believe that there is a plan behind the whole thing, which in turn implies that there must be a planner, a "mastermind" like Professor Moriarty pulling the strings. Moriarty himself is unobserved except for the results his actions bring. However, because most of life is interconnected, we can easily find patterns, even in the dark. William Sharpe, a Nobel laureate, used to say that any set of data would confess if you torture it enough. The same can be said for overanalyzing events for signs of conspiracy.

When an economic event happens, we are left with much the same feeling. The collapse of a currency, or the 1997 events in Southeast Asia, is so sudden and widespread that it is difficult to imagine that such a thing could happen by itself. The Malaysian Prime Minister will blame currency speculators rather than the financial imbalances in his own system. Leaders often have a difficult time admitting that they are not in control of their financial system. However, believers in free markets also have a hard time believing that the free market does not always know what is best, and they too can overreact to events.

Whenever hard times come, and perceptions of uncertainty rise, people begin to lose their faith in free-market systems. However, uncertainty is *always* a part of a free market. In fact, any process that allows its members freedom while maintaining an overall structure needs uncertainty in order to function. The uncertainty is the source of innovation and adaptation in the system. In a free market, uncertainty is a necessary and resultant condition of competition, the very defining characteristic of a free market. A free market cannot exist without it.

We also found that there are two areas that address these particular properties. In the sciences, complexity theory specifically studies self-organizing systems and has been able to model them effectively, using mathematics. In economics, the Austrian school has studied similar principles in economics for the past 100 years, but has done so in a qualitative way. Complexity theory now offers a scientific and mathematical basis for the insights of the Austrian school. Much of this book has dealt with this relationship, which has gone largely unexplored.

SELF-ORGANIZATION

A self-organizing process, we found, can exist in many different forms, but they all have common elements. The first is a *loose coupling* between the elements. Each element has a good deal of freedom, but because of the interrelationships, many of the elements are connected either directly or, more often, indirectly. We found that organization does not require direct connection for self-organization to occur. No "organization chart" is required either. If we think of the participants as buttons and the links as threads, we find that a phase change occurs when the ratio of threads to buttons crosses 0.50. That is, when half of the participants are directly linked, the size of the indirect links jumps from 12 percent of the participants to 80 percent. This phase change is important because it illustrates that an attempt to slowly create links will not achieve the benefits of self-organization gradually. Instead, when enough links are established, self-organization will occur suddenly.

Within the loose coupling, the elements are still independent, though they are constrained by their connections to the whole, which take the form of *rules* or natural law. However, predicting the activity of any one element is impossible. Still, the decentralized nature of the process allows it to be *innovative* and to evolve over time as its environment changes. The process can also *adapt* to a crisis—an ability that comes from the randomness or freedom of the individual participants. It introduces an element of *chance* into the system. We found that in evolutionary processes, as in genetic algorithms, chance plays an important role in the search process. In essence, solutions *compete* with each other for survival. Strangely, introducing randomness through competition makes the search process more structured and organized.

Finally, we found that complex systems are characterized by global structure and local randomness. Despite the independent nature of the individual participants, the loose coupling between the elements and the rules that govern those connections result in a global structure that is very stable. This *complex* system lies between structured processes (like machines) and completely chaotic ones (like a released balloon). A structured process is completely predictable, both locally and globally, but cannot adapt or grow. In fact, any disruption will cause a machine to break down. At the other extreme, a chaotic system is unstable at both the local and global levels. A change in its environment will cause it to jump to a completely different level.

Between these extremes exist complex systems that run without an organizer but adapt and innovate anyway, even as the individual elements can move about, randomly competing with one another, while still working toward the common goal. If any one element breaks down, the whole will continue to function. This is why complexity is so common in nature. Complex systems survive.

Complex systems always operate in a high state of uncertainty. This uncertainty cannot be eliminated because the individual elements cannot be predicted. The lack of predictability at the local level gives a complex system its global stability. Complexity needs uncertainty even as it generates more uncertainty.

AUSTRIAN ECONOMICS

The Austrian school has long felt that individuals operating in a free market and acting in their own self-interest will spontaneously organize because parts of society are dependent on the other participants in some way. They are linked by overlapping objectives and overlapping knowledge. Each individual subjectively interprets the common stock of knowledge and retains only the part that is personally relevant. However, the group as a whole has more knowledge than any one individual could ever have. As a result, the whole knows more than the sum of the parts. The Austrians contend that this decentralized stock of knowledge is more efficient at running a free market than a centralized system because no one individual or committee could know more than the whole. Because no one is in charge, there is often a feeling that things are out of control, particularly when hard times come.

The participants have overlapping goals that either conflict or cooperate with one another. Goals that cooperate show the interdependence of individuals. Goals that conflict come from competition for either resources or goods. Competition generates uncertainty as individual elements, particularly entrepreneurs, search for solutions to the problems and needs posed by society. There must be cooperation even among competitors, so rules are needed. These rules, once agreed on, become laws. In a free society, rules generally place limits on what is proper while giving individuals freedom to operate within the rules. In this way, free society operates like a game. Games have rules, but they allow for infinite variety and competition, which make a good game interesting. A structured society—for example, socialism—gives commands. Individuals are told what to do, rather than what they cannot do. This limits their ability to innovate and adapt, or to contribute creatively to the whole.

Free markets offer numerous benefits. For individuals, free markets offer opportunity. Because of the freedom each person has, there is potential for profit for everyone. There is also mobility. Anyone can start poor and become wealthier, even as the wealthy can become poor. Because everyone has opportunity, the whole market is offered stability.

Unfortunately, there is a price to pay for having these benefits. There can never be justice in the utopian manner. There will always be some who have an advantage through either birth or political power. In a free society, as long as individuals do not violate the freedom of others, they are free to do as they wish. Each free society has laws that protect the rights of individuals. Individual freedom is guaranteed, and all persons have equal rights. Unfortunately, there are no economic guarantees, and there can never be equal sharing of wealth. A free society has a duty to protect the very poor and disabled and to ensure a minimum standard of living. No one is guaranteed more.

The price of the free market is uncertainty. Because the individual elements are free to do what they wish, it is impossible to predict what any one person will do, or what day-to-day events will happen. Everyone has a different stock of knowledge and interprets it in a subjective way. Imbalances then develop in the economy, and the results are overproduction and, eventually, a crisis. Stability does not bring equilibrium, nor does it give us the "best of all possible worlds." Inevitably, economic conditions deteriorate as the excesses of the previous cycle reach a breaking point. Because of its decentralized nature, a free market can search for a solution, but a reasoned and fruitful search is difficult to manage in the midst of the crisis. There is always a cry for our leaders to *do something,* even though their understanding of the problem is probably not much better than ours. The most frequent solution—to take control by limiting the freedom of individuals—effectively limits the system's ability to find its own solution. Thus, the "solution" often makes things worse.

We should be careful whom we blame and what actions we allow our leaders to take. In many developing nations, free markets are a new development. Neither the leaders nor their citizens may understand that uncertainty is the price for the benefits of capitalism. If they are unaware of this fact, they may impose more structure when the hard times come, inadvertently causing a reverse-phase change that removes the self-organizing nature of a free market. Likewise, in developed nations, we should not put so much faith in the free market as a tool of social justice. The price of a free market includes uneven distribution of wealth, while offering mobility in the social structure. There should be some redistribution to help the disadvantaged and the poor, but we cannot expect that a free market will ever be able to offer complete social justice.

Finally, we should be aware that freedom requires both co-operation *and* competition. If we overemphasize one at the expense of the other, we run the risk of sliding into the chaos of anarchy or the soulless society of socialism. We must keep this balance in mind whenever we implement new rules.

MORIARTY REVEALED

Uncertainty is the price we pay for the benefits of a free-market system. Now that we recognize the self-organizing nature of the process, we know who Moriarty is. We are being kept in the dark by an organizing force that is none other than ourselves. We have our own limited perspective, and our own concerns, but they are part of the whole of society, a collective organization of which we can be only vaguely aware. The uncertainty we experience is not merely a price, it is a necessary component of life in general. Life is uncertain. We can be certain of that. But uncertainty is necessary. Without it, we would not have the variety that gives life interest, and the opportunity that gives life meaning.

We are being kept in the dark by an organizing force—ourselves.

References

Aczel, A.D. *Fermat's Last Theorem.* New York: Delta, 1996.

Arthur, W.B. *Increasing Returns and Path Dependence in the Economy.* Ann Arbor: University of Michigan Press, 1994.

Bak, P. *How Nature Works.* New York: Springer-Verlag, 1996.

Black, F., and Scholes, M. "The Pricing of Options and Corporate Liabilities," *Journal of Political Economy,* May/June 1973.

Bauer, R.J., Jr. *Genetic Algorithms and Investment Strategies,* New York: Wiley, 1994.

Bayles, D., and Orland, T. *Art and Fear.* Santa Barbara: Capra Press, 1993.

Bernstein, P.L. *Against the Gods.* New York: Wiley, 1996.

Csikszentmihalyi, M. *Creativity.* New York: HarperCollins, 1996.

Csikszentmihalyi, M. *Flow.* New York: Harper & Row, 1990.

Darwin, C. *The Origin of Species by Means of Natural Selection.* London: Watts, 1859.

Darwin, C. "The stock market is a lottery. Thank goodness for that," *The Economist,* August 8, 1992.

Eigen, M., and Winkler, R. *Laws of the Game.* Princeton: Princeton University Press, 1981.

Ekeland, I. *The Broken Dice.* Chicago: The University of Chicago Press, 1993.

Ekeland, I. *Mathematics and the Unexpected.* Chicago: The University of Chicago Press, 1988.

Fink, R.A., Ward, T.B., and Smith, S.M. *Creative Cognition.* Cambridge: MIT Press, 1992.

Ghiselin, B. *The Creative Process.* Los Angeles: University of California Press, 1952.

Greaves, B.B., Ed. *Austrian Economics: An Anthology.* New York: The Foundation for Economic Education, 1996.

Hayek, F.A. *The Essence of Hayek*. C. Nishiyama and K. Leube, Eds. Stanford: Hoover Institution Press, 1984.

Hayek, F.A. *Individualism and Economic Order*. Chicago: The University of Chicago Press, 1948.

Hayek, F.A. *Law Legislation and Liberty, Volume I: Rules and Order*. Chicago: The University of Chicago Press, 1973.

Heap, S.H., Hollis, M., Lyons, B., Sugden, R., and Weale, A. *The Theory of Choice*. Cambridge, England: Blackwell, 1992.

Heap, S.H., and Varoufakis, Y. *Game Theory*. New York: Routledge, 1995.

Hodgson, G.M. *Economics and Evolution*. Ann Arbor: The University of Michigan Press, 1996.

Holland, J.H. *Hidden Order*. New York: Helix, 1995.

Kahneman, D., Slovic, P., and Tversky, A. *Judgement Under Uncertainty: Heuristics and Biases*. Cambridge, England: Cambridge University Press, 1982.

Kauffman, S.A. *The Origins of Order*. New York: Oxford University Press, 1993.

Kauffman, S.A. *At Home with the Universe*. New York: Oxford University Press, 1995.

Keynes, J.M. *The General Theory of Employment, Interest and Money*. London: Macmillan, 1936.

Klir, G.J., and Folger, T.A. *Fuzzy Sets, Uncertainty and Information*. Englewood Cliffs: Prentice Hall, 1988.

Kolata, G. "1-in-a-trillion coincidence, you say? Not really, experts find." *The New York Times*, February 27, 1990.

Krugman, P. *The Self-Organizing Economy*. Cambridge, England: Blackwell, 1996.

Makhnenko, A. *The State Law of the Socialist Countries*. Moscow: Progress, 1976.

Nesse, M.N., and Williams, G.C. *Why We Get Sick*. New York: Times Books, 1994.

O'Driscoll, G.P., Jr., and Rizzo, J.M. *The Economics of Time and Ignorance*. New York: Routledge, 1996.

Peters, E.E. *Chaos and Order in the Capital Markets, Second Edition.* New York: Wiley, 1996.

Peters, E.E. *Fractal Market Analysis.* New York: Wiley, 1994.

Prigogine, I. *The End of Certainty.* New York: The Free Press, 1997.

Schumpeter, J.A. *Essays.* New Brunswick: Transactions Publishers, 1991. (Orig. published 1951.)

Schumpeter, J.A. *The Theory of Economic Development.* New Brunswick: Transactions Publishers, 1996. (Orig. published 1934.)

Shacklee, G.L.S. *Time in Economics.* Westport: Greenwood Press, 1958.

Shand, S.H. *Free Market Morality.* New York: Routledge, 1990.

Shaw, B. *The Intelligent Woman's Guide to Socialism and Capitalism.* New York: Brentano's, 1928.

Singh, S. *Fermat's Enigma.* New York: Walker, 1997.

Thaler, R. *The Winner's Curse: Paradoxes and Anomolies of Economic Life.* Princeton: Princeton University Press, 1994.

Vanberg, V.J. *Rules and Choice in Economics.* New York: Routledge, 1994.

Wiener, N. *Invention: The Care and Feeding of Ideas.* Cambridge: MIT Press, 1994.

Index

213